AMERICAN RIGHTS

FREEDOM OF RELIGION

Tom Head

Facts On File, Inc.

Freedom of Religion

Facts On File, Inc.
132 West 31st Street
New York NY 10001

Library of Congress Cataloging-in-Publication Data
Head, Tom.
   Freedom of religion / Tom Head.
      p. cm. — (American rights)
   Includes bibliographical references and index.
   ISBN 0-8160-5664-1
   1. United States—Religion—History—Juvenile literature. 2. Freedom of religion—United States—Juvenile literature. I. Title. II. Series.
   BL2525.H42 2005
   323.44′2′0973—dc222004020547

Facts On File books are available at special discounts when purchased in bulk quantities for businesses, associations, institutions, or sales promotions. Please call our Special Sales Department in New York at (212) 967-8800 or (800) 322-8755.

You can find Facts On File on the World Wide Web at http://www.factsonfile.com

Text design by Erika K. Arroyo
Cover design by Pehrsson Design
Maps and graphs by Dale Williams

Printed in the United States of America

VB FOF 10 9 8 7 6 5 4 3 2 1

This book is printed on acid-free paper.

For Mom and Cappy

Contents

Acknowledgments

I would like to extend humble thanks to my editor, Nicole Bowen, and editorial assistant Laura Shauger for their kindness, patience, sense of structure, and attention to detail; to Tracy Bradbury, for introducing me to this exciting project in the first place; and especially to my family, for their love and support.

Introduction

People often say, "You have a right to your opinion." What gives someone the right to have an opinion? Somebody might answer this question by saying that the government gives people the right to have an opinion. Does this mean that if someone lived in a country where some opinions were illegal, he or she would not have a right to an opinion?

Five hundred years ago, the answer would have been yes as far as most people were concerned. Although many governments had given certain rights to their citizens, governments had the power to award or not to award those rights as they saw fit. If a government passed laws banning certain opinions, many people probably would have said it was wrong because the government was being too cruel or too controlling, but most people would have believed that the government still technically had the right to do so.

During a period in Europe called the Enlightenment, which took place during the 17th and 18th centuries, various political thinkers started to argue that people had *natural* rights—rights they were born with, whether governments recognized those rights or not. The United States was the first country specifically established on the basis of the principle of natural rights and their guarantee. As Thomas Jefferson (1743–1826) wrote in the Declaration of Independence:

We hold these truths to be self-evident, that all men are created equal, that they are endowed by their Creator with certain unalienable Rights, that among these are Life, Liberty, and the pursuit of

Happiness. That to secure these rights, Governments are instituted among Men, deriving their just powers from the consent of the governed, that whenever any Form of Government becomes destructive of these ends, it is the Right of the People to alter or to abolish it.

At the time Jefferson wrote these words in 1776, most people would have actually disagreed with them. People living in the 18th century had been taught that their government came from God and that their rights came from the government. Jefferson argued that their rights came from God and their government came from their own decision to have a government. Furthermore, he argued that the main purpose of an ideal government was not to grow, or conquer, or grow richer, but to protect the basic rights that its citizens had already been born with. This was a dangerous idea. It was—literally—revolutionary.

The Enlightenment was a movement of thinkers, so the first rights Jefferson wanted to see protected were the freedoms to believe whatever one wished to believe and to publish new ideas. Without those freedoms, no other natural rights could be protected—indeed, the dangerous idea of natural rights itself could be suppressed. In 1789, only 13 years after the Declaration of Independence was written, the U.S. government passed a new Bill of Rights to protect the natural rights of its citizens. The very first words of the Bill of Rights protect the freedom to believe and the freedom to publish new ideas:

Congress shall make no law respecting an establishment of religion, or prohibiting the free exercise thereof; or abridging the freedom of speech, or of the press . . .

This entire book is about the first 16 words of that paragraph, which protect the right of every citizen to exercise his or her religious beliefs. The government, which has no mind of its own and therefore cannot have beliefs (religious or otherwise), is prohibited from establishing any official religion. This sounds so simple in theory, yet in practice it is incredibly complicated. For example:

- What if someone's religious beliefs tell him or her to do something that is against the law?
- What if politicians pass a law against something that members of a specific religion do but claim that the law was not directed against a particular religion when it was passed?

- What if most people hold a religious belief and want the government to celebrate that belief in a special way?
- What if many of the founding fathers who wrote the Constitution also believed that public schools should teach Christian Bible study classes and begin each day with a prayer?
- What if someone is drafted to serve in a war but has religious beliefs that prohibit him or her from serving?

Politicians and legal scholars agree that the first 16 words in the Bill of Rights stand as a central part of American law, but it is rare to find any two people who completely agree on what those 16 words mean. This book will explain why.

Religious Freedom in the American Colonies

In the 16th century, the part of North America that would later become known as the United States had been settled primarily by the British, Dutch, French, and Spanish. Each of these four countries brought a unique flavor of Christianity to the future United States. The Spanish and the French, for example, brought their own culture and their Roman Catholic heritage, but it would be the Protestant Puritanism and Anglicanism of the British colonists that would dominate American religious culture.

NEW SPAIN AND NEW FRANCE

Many of North America's earliest explorers and most active conquerors hailed from Spain, but the most successful Spanish colonies were located in Central and South America. Spanish colonies in what would later become the United States were sparse, located primarily in Florida, California, and the Southwest.

Religious fervor strengthened the Spanish government's drive for conquest first at home and then abroad. It was under the leadership of Spain's devoutly religious monarchs that the infamous Spanish Inquisition drove Jews and Muslims from Spain. Spain became a unified Roman Catholic nation, and its particular version of the Inquisition was exceptionally harsh and allowed for very little oversight from the pope, the head of the Roman Catholic Church. Spanish political leaders next sought to bring Spanish rule and Catholic faith to the Americas by conquest and domination. Some members of Spain's Roman Catholic religious orders opposed their government's violent methods to convert

> "Our principal goal was to obtain, to influence, and to attract the peoples of the [Americas] in order to convert them to our holy Catholic faith, and to send to those islands and mainlands . . . God-fearing people to instruct the inhabitants and neighbors of those lands in the Catholic faith and to show them new customs."
>
> —*Queen Isabella (1451–1504) of Spain, 1504*

local populations, preferring to achieve conversion through more traditional missionary efforts.

French settlement of North America in the 16th century included what became Canada, most of what became the central United States, and territory along the Mississippi River, including Louisiana. French motives for secular (nonreligious) conquest and religious conversion were more clearly separate than those of the Spanish, and its secular conquests were generally far less bloody than those of the Spanish. Although France and Spain shared a Roman Catholic religious establishment, that commitment did not prevent the two nations from coming into violent conflict. In fact, the first Spanish settlement in the future United States—St. Augustine, Florida, founded in 1595—was the result of a Spanish raid on an existing French settlement, which had been used as a port by French warships intercepting Spanish supplies.

Although their explorers can be credited for mapping much of the future United States, neither Spain nor France were able to colonize North American territory as effectively as the British did. With the Louisiana Purchase of 1803, France's North American presence retreated up to its northernmost outposts, in Canada. Spain ceded its

Although most English colonists were Protestants, Catholicism was heavily represented among colonists in New Spain, including in the region that would become the southwestern United States. In this 20th-century photograph, a group of New Mexico Catholics march in honor of a saint. *(Library of Congress, Prints and Photographs Division [LC-USF34-037119-D])*

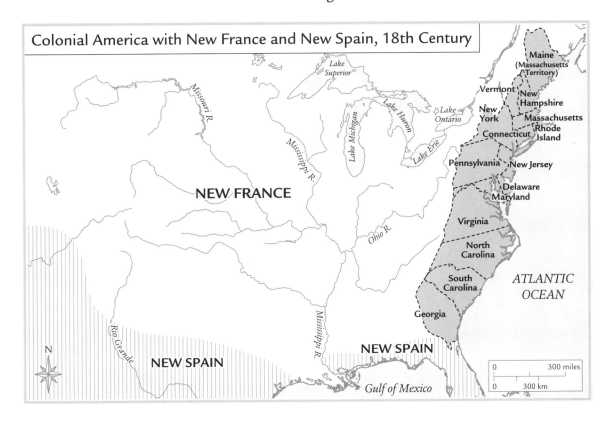

Colonial America with New France and New Spain, 18th Century

North American colonies to the United States and to Mexico following the Mexican War of Independence (1810–1821).

PURITANISM IN MASSACHUSETTS

In contrast to the Roman Catholic colonists from Spain and France, early English settlers were Protestants. They were either Anglicans (members of the Church of England, a government church that had broken with the Catholic Church but retained much of its liturgy, or church service format and tradition) or Puritans (dissenters who wanted to "purify" the Church of England of its Roman Catholic influences). Any Puritans in England who taught doctrines contrary to that of the Church of England were subject to legal restrictions, and many looked to the new American colonies as a possible haven.

It was a particular group of Puritans, known as the Pilgrims, who were the first English to risk the dangerous transcontinental

A group of English Puritans known as the Pilgrims braved a long and dangerous ocean voyage to settle in the area that would later become known as Massachusetts. *(Library of Congress, Prints and Photographs Division [LC-USZ62-4060])*

"We must delight in each other . . . mourn together, labor, and suffer together, always having before our eyes our Commission and Community in the work, our Community as members of the same body, so [that as] we keep the unity of the spirit in the bond of peace, the Lord will be our God and delight to dwell among us as his own people. . . . Consider that we shall be as a City upon a Hill, the eyes of all people are upon us; so that if we shall deal falsely with our God in this work we have undertaken and so cause him to withdraw his present help from us, we shall be made a story and a byword through the world."

—*John Winthrop, 1630*

voyage to unsettled territory on religious grounds. Staunch opponents of traditional Anglicanism, the Pilgrims had formed their own churches in England but were harassed by the government. They attempted to escape to Holland three times; arrested on their first two attempts, they succeeded on their third attempt in 1609. For various reasons—political, economic, and religious—the Pilgrims came to believe that Holland would not be a suitable long-term home for their religious movement, and they began to make plans to journey to America. They returned to England in 1620, where they quietly began a difficult 10-week voyage to the American coast aboard a ship they called the *Mayflower.*

They settled in Plymouth, Massachusetts, as a British colony, but their struggles had not ended. The *Mayflower* passengers suffered excruciating casualties: Fifty of the original 102 Pilgrims died by the end of their first winter in the colony, due primarily to lack of food. The colony survived on good fortune and the charity of local Native American tribes; Tisquantum (Squanto) (1590–1622), a member of the Patuxet tribe who had learned English while working as a guide for earlier European explorers, helped the Pilgrims grow crops and locate necessary resources. The new colony survived but remained small and would eventually be incorporated

THE ANTINOMIAN CONTROVERSY

The idea of heresy (unconventional religious opinion) trials in the United States may seem odd today, but such events were not particularly uncommon in 17th-century Massachusetts. The so-called Antinomian Controversy began in 1636 when Anne Hutchinson (1591–1643), a religious leader, started preaching in Boston. Her theology was extremely popular and attracted a considerable segment of the Massachusetts population, but it was very unconventional by Puritan standards. Hutchinson held that the authority of the Bible was secondary to personal religious experiences and that moral or immoral behavior did not necessarily indicate a person's relationship with God. The latter belief—referred to as the heresy of *antinomianism* (*anti* means "against" and *nomos* means "law")—gave a name to the controversy over her teachings, though the real scandal had more to do with her status as a woman preacher boldly objecting to the Puritan doctrines of Massachusetts.

Her heresy trial was held in 1637. Hutchinson was able to defend herself impressively against the criticisms of Massachusetts governor John Winthrop. Outmatched, Winthrop ended the debate by abruptly stating that he refused to debate theology any further with a woman. Hutchinson was found guilty and expelled from Massachusetts. Her followers were subject to religious persecution. She took up residence in the more liberal neighboring colony of Rhode Island. In 1639, Massachusetts leaders offered a partial apology for their behavior by granting amnesty to all Antinomians, provided that they "[carry] themselves peacefully."

While this ended the Antinomian Controversy itself, hostility toward Hutchinson and her followers continued in Massachusetts. For her part, Hutchinson's next few years were miserable; she suffered a miscarriage in 1638, her husband died in 1642, and she was murdered along with 10 of her children in a Native American raid in 1643. Puritan leaders in Massachusetts wrote at the time that her punishment came at the hands of God.

Seventeen years later, however, Puritan leaders dealt a more earthly punishment on one of Hutchinson's supporters. Mary Dyer (1591–1660) began to offend Massachusetts leaders during the Antinomian Controversy, and she fled to Rhode Island during the ensuing persecution. After converting to Quakerism (a Christian tradition that favors personal relationships with God) in 1650, she attempted to return to Massachusetts to preach. During her first three visits, she was imprisoned; on her fourth visit, in 1660, she was executed.

into a larger colony that had also begun to settle in the area—the Massachusetts Bay Colony.

Like the Plymouth colony, the Massachusetts Bay Colony was founded by Puritan refugees from England. While escaping from religious persecution, both colonies also sought to establish a government explicitly based on religious principles. John Winthrop (1588–1649), remembered today as the first governor of Massachusetts, led a group of settlers into Massachusetts in 1630 to establish what he called a "city upon a hill," an example of Puritan Christian government that he hoped would serve as a model for other governments throughout the world.

In colonial Massachusetts, religious offenses were therefore treated the same as secular offenses. The same laws that made murder and theft crimes also made blasphemy (speech that is regarded as offensive toward God) a crime. The same regulations that estab-

Puritans who led the Salem witch trials believed that some women, whom they called "witches," were evil and possessed dangerous supernatural powers. *(Library of Congress, Prints and Photographs Division [LC-USZ62-485])*

THE SALEM WITCH TRIALS

In 1692, when several girls and young women were discovered screaming blasphemously, experiencing seizures, and playing fortune-telling with a crystal ball, the residents of Salem, Massachusetts, blamed satanic intervention—specifically, evil witches. A local minister named Samuel Parris (1653–1720) saw this as an opportunity to rid the town of evil, declaring that it was overrun by a conspiracy of satanic witches who should be brought to justice. During the year, almost 200 Salem residents—many of them Parris's political enemies—were arrested, and 20 were executed. Trials generally did not rely on physical evidence, and in this case, they did not need to; local officials were able to rely on the panic and fear that had overtaken Salem.

Massachusetts governor Sir William Phips (1651–1693), who had approved the original trials, was stunned by reports of their outcomes. In fall 1692, he abolished the local courts responsible for the trials and established a new court to try the remaining witchcraft cases, all of which ended in acquittals. Over time, all surviving "witches" were released from prison and paid reparations by Massachusetts. The trials were regarded as an embarrassment to Massachusetts's Puritan government, and they have served to this day as an example of the dangers that can arise when religious frenzy supercedes—or determines—the rule of law.

lished the structure of government also mandated church attendance. Control over government decisions was democratic, but only confirmed church members were allowed to participate in decision making. Even within Protestant Christianity, unorthodox religious beliefs—such as those expressed by Anne Hutchinson (1591–1643) during the Antinomian Controversy (1636–37)—were subject to criminal prosecution. Enforcement of Massachusetts's religious laws reached its height during the Salem witch trials of 1692, which resulted in 19 executions.

On the other hand, Massachusetts leaders were not always unkind to religious minorities. Their goal was generally not to enforce uniform internal beliefs among the individual colonists but rather to protect the general beliefs of their community. Private religious expression was seldom punished, the emphasis instead being placed on public religious movements that threatened to disrupt Massachusetts's social harmony. Massachusetts gave relatively little power to the church as an institution. Because Puritans considered all human beings to be equal before God, ministers were not granted the sort of special legal status provided to them in England.

During the early 1700s, Massachusetts began to become more open to other religious traditions and the experiment in strict Puritan government was largely abandoned. The Massachusetts Constitution of 1780 guaranteed religious freedom to all of its citizens, "provided [that they] doth not disturb the public peace or obstruct others in their religious worship." In 1821, Massachusetts became the last state to formally end its involvement in religious affairs.

THE CHURCH OF ENGLAND IN AMERICA

The first permanent British colony in North America was founded in Jamestown, Virginia, in 1607. The British hoped this colony and others like it would slow the expansion of Roman Catholicism in the New World, which had begun in the colonies of New France and New Spain.

Virginia was a traditional Anglican colony, and its leaders were loyal to the Church of England. The Church of England was founded in 1534 when King Henry VIII (1491–1547), seeking a divorce, which was prohibited at the time under Catholicism, broke official ties between the British church and the Roman Catholic Church, based at the Vatican. During Henry's reign, the newly created Anglican Church was essentially Catholic in its customs, beliefs, and organization. His daughter, Queen Elizabeth I (1533–1603), however, defined the civic role of the Anglican faith. The Church of England had both Catholic and Protestant elements: It was Protestant inasmuch as it did not accept the pope's authority (the British monarch became head of the Church), but Catholic by tradition. Elizabeth sought to preserve both of these elements in the new church. In England Puritans, who objected to the church's more Catholic tendencies and sought a more emphatically Protestant church, were subject to various legal restrictions under British law (they were, for example, forbidden from holding public office). So, likewise, were Roman Catholics.

Far across the ocean, North America's geographical distance from England made it a haven for religious minorities. The British government, for its part, did little to counterbalance this trend with a strong Anglican presence. The American colonies were not provided with their own bishop until well into the 18th century, and they were forced to rely on long-distance supervision from the bishop of London. This meant that the colonies could not ordain their own priests and had to rely on the small number of priests who chose to make the costly and dangerous voyage across the Atlantic Ocean to America, where the standard of living was much lower and the culture sometimes hostile to Anglicanism.

NEW NETHERLAND AND THE DUTCH REFORMED CHURCH

What is now New York State began as a fur trading colony founded by the Dutch West India Company in 1624. This colony—known at the time as New Netherland, with its principal settlement at New Amsterdam on the island of Manhattan—did not begin as a particularly religious colony, but its religious culture was heavily affected by a growing population of Dutch Reformed Protestants and the administration of a deeply religious governor named Peter Stuyvesant (1592–1672). Over a period of decades, the Dutch Reformed Church grew in New Netherland and became an essential part of its culture.

The Dutch administration of New Netherland did not last for long, however, as the colony was soon surrounded by much larger and more influential British colonies. In 1664, a small British fleet sailed into New Amsterdam's harbor and demanded a surrender. The 2,000 Dutch traders who made up the colony agreed, and New Netherland was promptly renamed New York (after the duke of York, brother of King Charles II and later himself King James II). Out of respect for the original colony, the British invaders chose to allow Dutch Reformed churches in New York to continue to operate without fear of censure.

Original Religious Establishments in the Thirteen Colonies, 1630–1763

Maine
(Massachusetts
Territory)

New Hampshire

Massachusetts

New York

Rhode Island

Connecticut

Pennsylvania

New Jersey

Delaware

Maryland

Virginia

North Carolina

South Carolina

Georgia

ATLANTIC
OCEAN

Lake Superior

Lake Huron

Lake Michigan

Lake Ontario

Lake Erie

Mississippi R.

Ohio R.

Mississippi R.

Gulf of Mexico

N

Legend:
- Anglican
- Dutch Reformed
- Non-Denominational
- Puritan
- Quaker
- Roman Catholic

0   300 miles
0   300 km

Separation of church and state did not exist in the earliest North American colonies. Even the most liberal colony, Rhode Island, affirmed Christianity as its official religion, and most colonies had laws prohibiting blasphemy and preventing non-Christians from serving in political office.

Like most loyal Anglican colonies, Virginia supported its local priests with government funds and actively discouraged its Puritans and Roman Catholics from forming churches. After the Glorious Revolution of 1688–89—in which a Catholic British monarch (James II) was deposed—Virginia began to give greater leeway to Puritanism, even as hostility toward Roman Catholics began to increase.

Although colonial Virginia generally allowed greater freedom in religious exercise than did Massachusetts, it had a national British church whose priests were accorded special status. They were not, however, given much power; because so few priests were available in America, and no bishops had been appointed, real authority over church decisions generally rested with vestries (committees of laypersons), who had the power to hire and fire priests at will. This left Anglican priests in a precarious position, particularly as the era of the American Revolution began and anti-British sentiment began to spread. By the end of the American Revolution in 1781, the Church of England had lost all official power in the United States.

After the revolution, Anglicans living in the United States were granted the power to appoint their own bishops and promptly reformed as the Episcopal Church of the United States of America. Although the U.S. Episcopal Church is now independent and receives no government support, church leaders still answer to the archbishop of Canterbury, the traditional leader of the Church of England.

ROMAN CATHOLICISM IN MARYLAND

Roman Catholics faced legal persecution and public discrimination in the newly Protestant culture of 17th-century Britain. George Calvert (1580–1632), a powerful adviser to King Charles I (1600–49), surprised many—and lost a great deal of political power—when he announced in 1625 that he was Roman Catholic and had only been conforming to the public rituals of the Church of England (as many Catholics and other non-Anglicans of his time did to avoid persecution). He immediately used his public image and political clout to lobby on behalf of British Catholics, petitioning the king for a colony in the New World dedicated specifically to Catholics.

After failed attempts to establish colonies in Newfoundland and Virginia, Calvert petitioned for land immediately north of Virginia. He died before the king approved his request, so his sons,

> "On the day of the Annunciation of the Most Holy Virgin Mary in the year 1634, we celebrated the mass for the first time . . . in this part of the world. After we had completed the sacrifice, we took upon our shoulders a great cross, which we had hewn out of a tree, and . . . we erected a trophy to Christ the Saviour, humbly reciting, on our bended knees, the Litanies of the Sacred Cross, with great emotion."
>
> —*Friar Andrew White, describing a service held by Roman Catholic settlers en route to Maryland*

Cecilius and Leonard Calvert, administered the new colony, named Maryland (named after Henrietta Maria, Charles I's Roman Catholic wife). Although the colony was created as a Catholic refuge, Protestants were welcome—indeed, the vast majority of early colonists were Protestant.

The Act of Toleration of 1649 officially granted full legal rights to all Christian citizens living in Maryland who did not deny the doctrine of the Trinity (the essence of God as expressed in the persons of the Father, Son, and Holy Spirit), in an attempt to prevent a Protestant revolt in the colony as a religious-based power struggle developed. Protestants attempted coups in the early 1640s and again in the mid-1650s, but the Calverts were able to reassert control in both cases. Until the late 1680s, Maryland was a rare refuge for Roman Catholics and Protestants alike.

The reign of King James II (1633–1701) changed British attitudes toward Roman Catholics. James, a convert to the Catholic faith, ascended to the throne in 1685 and immediately began a series of aggressive reforms. While many of the reforms represented a well-intentioned attempt to improve the lives of British Catholics, his stubbornness and tendency to ignore the rule of law outraged the British public and in just a few years turned them against both James and his faith. He was overthrown in the Glorious Revolution of 1688–89 and replaced by his Protestant daughter, Queen Mary II (1662–94), and her husband, King William III (1650–1702) of the Netherlands.

William and Mary would be remembered as more tolerant than many of their predecessors, but they were as susceptible as any to the wave of anti-Catholicism felt by Britain following the disastrous reign of James II. They placed Maryland under direct royal control in 1691, removing the Calverts from power and establishing the Church of England in that colony. Roman Catholics would remain a persecuted minority in most of the United States until the American Revolution.

ROGER WILLIAMS AND THE RHODE ISLAND COLONY

Like many 17th-century Puritan ministers living in England, Roger Williams (1603–83) sought citizenship in Massachusetts. He arrived there in 1630 but found it little more to his liking than England.

When offered a position as pastor of a congregation in Salem, he turned down the offer on the grounds that the church had not adequately severed its ties with the Church of England. He eventually took it in 1633, but he used his pulpit to argue on behalf of his beliefs regarding church and state. He felt that government officials should not legislate religious matters, that church and state should be entirely separate, and that churches in Salem, in particular, should resist colonial authority. He was called before the Massachusetts General Court in 1635, where he was promptly expelled for stating "new and dangerous opinions against the authority of magistrates."

Accompanied by a small band of devoted followers, Williams traveled south and purchased land from the Narragansett Indians. He founded the city of Providence in 1636, then traveled to England in 1642 to secure a colonial charter. His efforts were successful, and the tiny colony of Rhode Island was formed. It soon became a haven for Jews, Roman Catholics, and people of other oppressed religious groups who had been made to feel unwelcome in other colonies.

One of these groups was the Baptists, a sect that had originated in England during the first years of the 17th century. Like Puritans, Baptists objected to the Church of England, but unlike most Puritans, Baptists objected to all state-sponsored expression of religion: They were strongly opposed to the concept of national churches, which they felt corrupted religious life. As the name implies, Baptists also held distinctive beliefs about baptism. They believed that a baptism had to reflect a conscious act of faith in order to be valid, and on this basis they objected to infant baptism (a common practice in both the Church of England and Puritan churches). They also held that baptism ought to be performed by full immersion rather than by a sprinkling of water. Many Baptists had traveled to Massachusetts in an effort to avoid the jurisdiction of the Church of England, only to find that Puritan churches there were no more amenable to their practices than the Anglicans. Many migrated to Rhode Island, which was soon regarded as a Baptist colony.

Until the revolutionary era, Rhode Island was the only colony to have no official state religion. Although it was seen as a strange, marginal community of outcasts at the time, it was the only colony to fully affirm both of the freedoms later guaranteed by the First Amendment's clauses on religion; free exercise of religion and separation of church and state.

"[Religious] conscience is found in all mankind, more or less: in Jews, Turks, Papists, Protestants, pagans. . . . Sir, I must be humbly bold to say that 'tis impossible for any man or men to maintain their Christ by their sword and to worship a true Christ, to fight against all consciences opposite to theirs, and not to fight against God in some of them."

—*Roger Williams, in a letter to Massachusetts governor John Endicott, 1651*

PENNSYLVANIA'S "HOLY EXPERIMENT"

As the son of a legendary British admiral, William Penn (1644–1718) was one of the most powerful and controversial figures of 17th-century England. After attending Oxford University, he was drawn to Puritanism and then to the Religious Society of Friends (Quakers), to which he converted. He became known as a prolific author of Quaker theological and devotional works, and as was the custom for vocal Quakers in Britain at the time, he faced arrest for expressing his beliefs. Yet every time he was arrested, Penn managed to avoid conviction; in one case, in fact, members of a jury had been commanded by the judge to render a guilty verdict or suffer criminal charges themselves. Despite the threat, they found Penn not guilty. He was so well liked and had such powerful political connections that he seemed almost immune to Britain's anti-Quaker persecution, which he campaigned against vigorously.

Founded in 1652 by George Fox (1624–91), the Religious Society of Friends faced persecution since its inception. The very name *Quaker* comes from an exchange between Fox and an English judge, which took place upon Fox's arrest for disturbing the peace. "I bid thee tremble before the word of God," Fox is reputed to have said, to which the judge replied, "I bid thee quake before the law." Quakerism is distinguished primarily by three characteristics: belief in personal revelation (the "Inner Light"), opposition to violence of all kinds, and a refusal to submit to earthly authorities. Quakers fleeing England often fared no better in the United States; when two Quakers, Mary Fisher and Ann Austin, arrived in Massachusetts in 1656, they were immediately arrested and shipped back. Other prominent Quaker figures, such as Mary Dyer (discussed earlier in this chapter), were executed for their heresies.

It soon became clear to Penn that Quakers needed a haven, and the New World seemed the most plausible location for one. The government of Britain owed him money, and he was able to barter this debt into a large plot of land west of Delaware as payment. This

William Penn founded Pennsylvania as a Quaker colony and established religious liberty as one of its basic principles.
(Library of Congress, Prints and Photographs Division [LC-USZ62-106735])

new colony, Pennsylvania, was founded in 1681 on Quaker principles. It had no established church, tolerated all faiths, sponsored no state militia, and maintained friendly terms with Native Americans of the region. It soon became known as a haven for religious minorities, surpassing even Rhode Island in its diversity. German Lutherans and Dutch Reformed Christians settled in the colony alongside Quakers, Baptists, Roman Catholics, Jews, Unitarians, and others.

In 1699, Penn formally gave up his claim to the colony and made it self-governing. Although it gradually drifted away from its Quaker principles—for example, establishing military draft laws during the American Revolution and later declaring itself to be neutral on religious matters—it has been and continues to be among the most religiously diverse states in the United States.

THE END OF THE COLONIAL ERA

As the 17th century gave way to the 18th, the American colonies became more open to commerce and cultural exchange. Massachusetts, its leaders still shamed by the Salem witchcraft trials, began to be less strict in its application of religious laws. Also, across the colonies, the Great Awakening, a surge in personal and congregational piety, began to emerge during the 1720s and continued until the revolutionary era. With the Awakening, American Christian culture tended to place greater emphasis on personal religious experiences and less emphasis on institutional churches, which were viewed with gradually increasing suspicion. The Baptists, once a small sect in Rhode Island, began to emerge as a major national force opposing all state-sponsored churches. And the Church of England, which represented the very concept of a state-sponsored church, became less and less popular as revolutionary sentiment began to catch on.

The 17th century was influential in determining how America's colonial religious cultures would relate to England's, but it was not until the 18th century that the colonies began to develop a national religious character. The almost uniquely American rebellion against official creeds and state-sponsored churches would later take hold in the American Revolution and be forever codified in the First Amendment of the U.S. Constitution.

"That there is such a thing as conscience, and the liberty of it, in reference to faith and worship towards God, must not be denied, even by those that are most scandalized at the ill use some seem to have made of such pretenses."

—*William Penn,
A Persuasive to
Moderation to Church
Dissenters in Prudence
and Conscience (1686)*

2

The Freedom of Conscience

The American right to freedom of religion is protected by the First Amendment to the U.S. Constitution. The American court system now uses this amendment to restrict both the U.S. and state governments from passing laws that prohibit religious expression or contribute to the establishment of a national religion. This has not always been the case.

When the First Amendment was originally proposed in 1789, it amounted to a guarantee by the U.S. Congress to regulate itself. It was only relevant at a federal level, as it did not yet apply to state law, and there was no practical way of enforcing it because the U.S. Supreme Court had not yet established the power to strike down unconstitutional laws. Although the First Amendment has always been a guiding principle of U.S. law, it did not reach its current level of power until well into the 20th century. It achieved that power step by step, through a long series of catastrophic events and groundbreaking judicial interpretations.

THE ROOTS OF THE FIRST AMENDMENT

The concept of a bill of rights was not unfamiliar to the American revolutionaries. English law was based on two bills of rights, the Magna Carta of 1215 and the English Bill of Rights of 1689. While the Magna Carta restricted the power of government and established basic rules of tax and property law, it did not guarantee the sort of individual liberties that one generally associates with bills of rights today. It was the more modern English Bill of Rights which strengthened the criminal law process and granted free speech rights to members of Parliament, that ultimately served as a loose model for the U.S. Constitution and Bill of Rights. Neither declaration, however, explicitly protected the individual right to free religious expression.

When Virginia lawmaker George Mason (1725–92) drafted a Declaration of Rights in 1776, several months before the United States declared its independence from Great Britain, he included a provision specifically protecting the "free exercise of religion." The tone of this rights declaration not only affirmed the belief that all people had natural rights, whether a government chose to acknowledge them or not—a concept enshrined in the Declaration of Independence, written several months later by Thomas Jefferson (1743–1826)—but explicitly outlined what some of those rights were. One of those rights was the "free exercise of religion, according to the dictates of conscience."

Thomas Jefferson was an early advocate of religious freedom and insisted that it be protected in the Bill of Rights. *(Library of Congress, Prints and Photographs Division [LC-USZCN4-190])*

Yet Virginia had been founded with an Anglican (Church of England) religious establishment (state religion). The idea of religious establishment in general—and the Church of England in particular—became extremely unpopular during the American Revolution, and some sought to clearly establish that Virginia no longer had an official church. Chief among these people was Jefferson, who drafted an Act for Establishing Religious Freedom in 1779. The bill, extremely controversial at the time, clearly prevented the state government from having any sort of religious establishment and included a lengthy philosophical argument in favor of secular government. The bill took seven years to pass and faced stern opposition from renowned patriot Patrick Henry

> "[R]eligion, or the duty which we owe to our Creator and the manner of discharging it, can be directed by reason and conviction, not by force or violence; and therefore, all men are equally entitled to the free exercise of religion, according to the dictates of conscience; and that it is the mutual duty of all to practice Christian forbearance, love, and charity towards each other."
>
> —*Virginia Declaration of Rights (1776)*

> "[T]o compel a man to furnish contributions of money for the propagation of opinions which he disbelieves is sinful and tyrannical [and] . . . to suffer the civil magistrate to intrude his powers into the field of opinion and to restrain the profession or propagation of principles on supposition of their ill tendency is a dangerous fallacy, which at once destroys all religious liberty[.]"
>
> —*Virginia Act for Establishing Religious Freedom (1786)*

(1736–99) at a time when Jefferson himself was overseas serving as ambassador to France. James Madison (1751–1836) defended the bill in his stead, and it was ultimately approved by the legislature in 1786. By specifically protecting the right to free religious exercise and repudiating all government establishment of religion, the Virginia legislature set a precedent that the federal government would soon follow.

THE CONSTITUTIONAL DEBATE

During the American Revolution, the United States was governed under the Articles of Confederation. These articles did not guarantee religious freedom, but there was little need to do so—the federal government under the articles was in effect a cooperative association of independent states and had little power to restrict religion.

When the Constitutional Convention assembled in 1787 to create a permanent set of resolutions to define the powers of the national government, many sought to guarantee religious freedom (as the Virginia statutes had) as part of a broader bill of rights. Supporters of the original draft of the Constitution produced by the convention argued that this was completely unnecessary in a democratic government, because Congress (which represented the will of the people) was asked, in effect, to restrict itself. The strength of the first version of the Constitution, as many saw it, was that it made no permanent claims and was subject to revision at any time. If "our [descendants] are bound by our constitutions," wrote Patriot and future dictionary author Noah Webster (1758–1843), "they are to all intents and purposes our slaves." The proposed Constitution was, however, supportive of religious liberty in the few religious issues it did address, such as banning religious tests and allowing elected officials to take affirmations rather than religious oaths. The Constitution was ratified by the necessary two-thirds majority of states in 1788, but five states—New York, North Carolina, Rhode Island, Vermont, and Virginia—withheld their ratification until later. One of the reasons for this was the Constitution's lack of a bill of rights. George Mason of Virginia, who had drafted the original 1776 Virginia Declaration of Rights, refused to sign the Constitution precisely for this reason.

The figure ultimately responsible for proposing the Bill of Rights was James Madison. Nicknamed "Father of the Constitution" for the central role he played in drafting it, he strongly supported the original, unamended (unaltered) Constitution. Madison was under great pressure from Thomas Jefferson (with whom he had worked to

THE BURKE-PAINE CONTROVERSY

Few debates from the revolutionary era sum up popular attitudes about religious establishment as well as those between British lawmaker Edmund Burke (1729–97) and American journalist Thomas Paine (1737–1809).

Burke was a moderate voice who had been a frequent advocate for American colonists during the prewar years but was stunned by the possibility of a bloody revolution. "I do not know how," he wrote, "to wish success to those whose victory is to separate us from a large and noble part of our empire. . . . No good can come of any event in this war to any virtuous interest."

Paine, for his part, is remembered today as one of the most eloquent prowar activists of his time. In a series of pamphlets titled *Common Sense* (1776), Paine drummed up popular support for the Revolution through both humor ("there is something very absurd in supposing a continent to be perpetually governed by an island") and pathos ("Hath your house been burnt? Hath your property been destroyed before your face? Are your wife and children destitute of a bed to lie on, or bread to live on? Have you lost a parent or child by [British] hands, and yourself the ruined and wretched survivor?").

The two would disagree in a more direct fashion in 1790, when the French Revolution prompted Burke to write what would become his masterpiece, a lengthy political treatise titled *Reflections on the Revolution in France* (1790). As part of his defense of the classical European system of government, Burke justified what he saw as the need for official church-state cooperation. Although he defended individual religious liberty, he still felt that a national church of some kind was necessary to preserve public morals, hold political leaders to a high ethical standard, and contribute to national culture. "[R]eligion," Burke wrote, "is the basis of civil society, and the source of all good." If the idea of a national church were abolished, "[n]o one generation could link with the other" and "[m]en would become little better than the flies of a summer."

In response to Burke's *Reflections,* Paine wrote *The Rights of Man* (1791–92). He regarded Burke's arguments on behalf of church-state unity as naive at best, arguing that "[by] the connection which Mr. Burke recommends . . . a sort of mule-animal, capable only of destroying, and not breeding up, is produced, called the Church established by Law." Paine believed that "[a]ll religions are in their nature kind and benign, and united with principles of morality." Only government support of religion—with its implicit threat of force—could thoroughly corrupt it.

Even today, political scholars look back on Burke and Paine as examples of two parallel streams of thought that existed during the American Revolution. Edmund Burke represented a way of dealing with state religion that sought to preserve the status quo and the British national culture associated with it. Thomas Paine felt the status quo to be dangerous and restrictive and argued for what would become the American experiment: a secular government that made no attempt to establish or regulate religious life.

> "The legitimate powers of government extend to such acts only as are injurious to others. But it does me no injury for my neighbor to say there are twenty gods, or no god. It neither picks my pocket nor breaks my leg. . . . It is error alone which needs the support of government. Truth can stand by itself."
>
> —*Thomas Jefferson*, Notes on the State of Virginia *(1785)*

secure passage of Virginia's Act for Establishing Religious Freedom only a few years before) to propose a bill of rights guaranteeing that the federal government would be restricted by human rights standards at least as strict as those of Virginia. "The inconveniences" of not passing a bill of rights, Jefferson wrote in a 1789 letter to Madison, would be "permanent, afflicting, irreparable, [and] in constant progression from bad to worse." Madison eventually agreed and proposed a Bill of Rights in 1789, pacifying many of the Constitution's most vocal critics. The Bill of Rights did little more than that, however, because there was no practical way of enforcing it at the time.

Several years after successfully gaining passage of Thomas Jefferson's Virginia statute for religious freedom, James Madison proposed the U.S. Bill of Rights. *(Library of Congress, Prints and Photographs Division [LC-USZ62-16960])*

OATHS AND RELIGIOUS TESTS

"The Senators and Representatives before mentioned, and the Members of several State Legislatures, and all executive and judicial Officers, both of the United States and of the several States, shall be bound by Oath or Affirmation, to support this Constitution; but no religious Tests shall ever be required as a Qualification to any Office or public Trust under the United States."

—U.S. Constitution, Article VI, Clause 3

Even before the Bill of Rights was proposed, the Constitution included provisions addressing two controversial issues pertaining to religious freedom: oaths and religious tests.

The concept of religious oaths has a rich ceremonial history in American politics. Whether in a court of law or while taking the oath of office as president, a citizen is usually expected to place his or her right hand on the Bible and repeat a phrase that begins "I do solemnly swear. . . ." Even in the 18th century, however, there were many who disagreed with the idea of swearing oaths—especially Quakers, who were expressly forbidden from doing so. To accommodate such perspectives, the Constitution is carefully written never to require anyone to take an actual oath; one is always given the option of taking an "affirmation" instead, substituting the word *affirm* for *swear*. The use of the Bible as part of the process is also never mentioned in the Constitution; its use during the Oath of the Presidency is a voluntary practice that began with George Washington (1732–99).

Likewise, the authors of the Constitution felt the need to protect citizens from religious tests. In England, religious minorities such as Quakers, Roman Catholics, and Puritans were frequently forbidden from holding public office by the use of religious tests, which called on the citizen to state that his or her beliefs conformed to a national religious ideal. To protect the rights of religious minorities, the authors of the Constitution included a special provision specifically preventing the federal government from ever requiring officials to hold uniform beliefs.

THE RISE OF THE U.S. SUPREME COURT

In a scathing editorial written in 1788, lawmaker and war hero Alexander Hamilton described state bills of rights as being made up primarily of "volumes of aphorisms . . . which would sound much better in a treatise of ethics than in a constitution of government." Although he came to support the Bill of Rights over time much as Madison had, his original point stood. The Bill of Rights restricted Congress only inasmuch as Congress chose to be restricted by it. It was more an honor code than a legally binding agreement.

"It is apparent that the framers of the Constitution contemplated that instrument as a rule for the government of courts, as well as of the legislature. Why else does it direct the judges to take an oath to support it? . . . The particular phraseology of the Constitution of the United States confirms and strengthens the principle, supposed to be essential to all written constitutions, that a law repugnant to the constitution is void."

—*Chief Justice John Marshall (1755–1835) of the Supreme Court, from his majority opinion in* Marbury v. Madison *(1803)*

This changed in 1803 with the U.S. Supreme Court case of *Marbury v. Madison,* in which the Court deal with an administrative dispute that arose as Thomas Jefferson replaced John Adams (1735–1826) as president of the United States. Adams had appointed a court justice named James Marbury at the very end of his administration. Jefferson declared the appointment void, a point Marbury challenged in court. Marbury filed suit against James Madison—Jefferson's secretary of state—and attempted to convince the Supreme Court to order Madison to reinstate him under the Judiciary Act of 1789. The Supreme Court declared the Judiciary Act of 1789 unconstitutional and struck it down, establishing a power the Court had not previously possessed. For the first years of its existence, the Court was charged merely with interpreting existing laws. With the *Marbury v. Madison* precedent, it claimed the power to actually strike them down if they violated the Constitution or its amendments (changes)—though it would be another 76 years before this power was extended to the First Amendment's religion clauses in *Reynolds v. United States* (1879). Federal laws dealing with religion were extremely rare; it was nearly always state laws that addressed such issues, as in the case of Massachusetts (which, until 1821, was authorized to tax its citizens to pay for "public Protestant teachers of piety, religion, and morality").

Madison had declared in his original draft of the Bill of Rights that "no state shall violate the equal rights of conscience, or the freedom of the press, or the trial by jury in criminal cases," but the Senate struck down this portion out of concern that it could be seen as an infringement on the autonomy of individual states. For more than a century, the Bill of Rights applied only to federal law.

Chief Justice John Marshall first established the Supreme Court's power to strike down unconstitutional laws. *(Library of Congress, Prints and Photographs Division [LC-D416-29922])*

THE STATE GOVERNMENT OF MASSACHUSETTS BECOMES SECULAR

"It is the right as well as the duty of all men in society, publicly, and at stated seasons to worship the Supreme Being, the great Creator and Preserver of the universe. And no subject shall be hurt, molested, or restrained . . . for worshipping God in the manner and season most agreeable to the dictates of his own conscience . . . provided he doth not disturb the public peace, or obstruct others in their religious worship.

". . . [T]he legislature shall, from time to time, authorize and require, the several towns, parishes, precincts, and other bodies politic, or religious societies, to make suitable provision, at their own expense, for the institution of the public worship of God, and for the support and maintenance of public Protestant teachers of piety, religion, and morality, in all cases where such provisions shall not be made voluntarily. And the people of this commonwealth . . . invest their legislature with authority to enjoin upon all the subjects an attendance upon the instructions of the public teachers aforesaid, at stated times and seasons, if there be any on whose instructions they can conscientiously and conveniently attend."

—from Articles II and III of the
Massachusetts Constitution (1780)

As other states codified separation of church and state by adopting rights declarations during the 1770s and 1780s, Massachusetts held on to its colonial heritage as a religious state. There were two primary reasons for this.

The first was that Massachusetts had been explicitly established as a Puritan colony. When he drafted "A Model of Christian Charity" (1630), future Massachusetts governor John Winthrop described the Massachusetts Bay Colony as an attempt to "seek out a place of cohabitation and consortship under a due form of government both civil and ecclesiastical." Just as thinkers such as Jefferson envisioned the United States as an experiment in secular government, so did the founders of Massachusetts envision their state as an experiment in Christian government. "[W]e shall be as a city upon a hill," Winthrop wrote, as "the eyes of all people are upon us."

The second had to do with the kind of religious establishment that Massachusetts had. Although its colonial laws were very restrictive, Massachusetts was not connected to the Church of England or any other broad, international denominations. Its established faith was Congregationalist in that it gave a great deal of leverage to local churches, and later laws—such as the Constitution of 1780—made it possible for religious minorities such as Jews, Quakers, and Roman Catholics to live in the state and worship without breaking the law.

In 1821, Massachusetts became the last state to officially separate its government from religious matters. Lawmakers revised Articles I and III of the state's constitution to strike out al references to public funding of religion and added a clause stating that "all religious sects and denominations . . . shall be equally under the protection of the law." After almost 200 years, Winthrop's experiment in religious government had come to an end.

THE FOURTEENTH AMENDMENT AND THE INCORPORATION DOCTRINE

The bloody U.S. Civil War (1861–65) was a complex struggle that centered on slavery, but it was also influenced by competing ideas of what the proper relationship between the federal and state governments should be. When the country divided in two, the South revisited the language of the revolutionary-era Articles of Confederation, forming the Confederate States of America, while the North fought with the explicit goal of preserving the young constitutional republic.

The war ended with a crushing defeat for the South. The group of states that had defected from the United States, partly out of fear that President Abraham Lincoln (1809–65) would eventually interfere with the slavery-based economies of the South, had seen much of the fruits of those economies destroyed by war and the institution of slavery permanently abolished. Angry southerners passed "black codes" in order to restrict African Americans—and especially recently freed slaves—from holding full citizenship in their states, a policy that the U.S. government countered with the Fourteenth Amendment (1868) to the U.S. Constitution.

The Fourteenth Amendment stipulates that "No State shall make or enforce any law which shall abridge the privileges or immunities of citizens of the United States; nor shall any State deprive any person of life, liberty, or property, without due process of law; nor deny to any person within its jurisdiction the equal protection of the laws." African-American citizens, however, continued to face state-sponsored discrimination until well into the 20th century, when a series of new laws and Supreme Court rulings ended institutional segregation and gave citizens of all races the right to vote. In the midst of this civil rights movement, the Supreme Court took a second look at what *liberty* as described in the Fourteenth Amendment really meant. Did it refer to the Bill of Rights, or to another standard? In *Gitlow v. New York* (1925), the Supreme Court established that the Bill of Rights as a whole did, in fact, apply to state law under the Fourteenth Amendment under what was called the "incorporation doctrine." The incorporation doctrine holds that that the liberty protected by the Fourteenth Amendment refers, by definition, to a national standard of liberty—one which must logically incorporate the Bill

In the aftermath of the Civil War, Congress wrote the Fourteenth Amendment to prevent the defeated Confederate states from passing laws hostile toward African Americans. The Supreme Court would later cite this amendment when applying the First Amendment's religion clauses to state law. *(Library of Congress, Prints and Photographs Division [LC-USZ62-9706])*

of Rights, in order to grant all citizens "equal protection."

The Court first applied the incorporation doctrine to free religious exercise in *Cantwell v. Connecticut* (1940). Newton Cantwell, a Jehovah's Witness who distributed pamphlets door to door and recommended the purchase of books related to his tradition, was arrested by the state of Connecticut for selling books without a license. When the case reached the Supreme Court, it ruled in Cantwell's favor and argued that the state law violated the free exercise clause of the First Amendment. Although the precise argument

"The fundamental concept of liberty embodied in [the Fourteenth] Amendment embraces the liberties guaranteed by the First Amendment. The First Amendment declares that Congress shall make no law respecting an establishment of religion or prohibiting the free exercise thereof. The Fourteenth Amendment has rendered the legislatures of the states as incompetent as Congress to enact such laws."

—*Justice Owen Josephus Roberts (1875–1955) of the Supreme Court, from his majority ruling in* Cantwell v. Connecticut *(1940)*

behind the ruling is still considered controversial, the authority of the ruling—based on the belief that the U.S. Supreme Court can strike down state laws for violating the Bill of Rights—is not.

In the past two centuries, the First Amendment has transformed from a self-binding statement of legislative principles into one of the most basic and unassailable documents in American law. Although government officials often disagree over precisely how they should be interpreted, the First Amendment's firm guarantees of individual religious liberty and separation of church and state now apply to every U.S. citizen.

3

A Nation of Diverse Religions

From the time the American colonies were founded until the late 18th century, most Americans identified themselves as Protestants, and laws were written on the assumption that Protestantism would be the nation's common religion. Roman Catholics and other Christian minority groups faced persecution in most states. The only non-Christian faith that had established a solid presence in the United States was Judaism, and even Jews were not allowed to participate in most arenas of public life. It would have been entirely accurate to describe the United States as a Protestant Christian nation by law, statistics, and culture.

Since that time, the situation has changed dramatically. Presently, between 75 and 85 percent of the U.S. population identifies itself as Christian (and about one-third of American Christians identify as Roman Catholic). The remaining 15–25 percent is made up of millions of Jews, Muslims, Buddhists, and Hindus, and millions more who belong to smaller religions or to no religion at all. No single religion has complete power over U.S. public life, and Americans of any religious background can start a congregation or run for political office.

Each major non-Christian religious tradition has its own history in the United States. Most have progressed from isolation to acceptance, but one group of traditions has faced near elimination.

> "Through [the] decades since the liberalization of immigration policy in 1965 . . . [t]he United States has become the most religiously diverse nation on earth."
>
> —*Harvard University religion professor Diana Eck*, A New Religious America *(2000)*

NATIVE AMERICAN FAITH TRADITIONS

When Christopher Columbus (1451–1506) arrived in the Bahamas in 1492, he thought that he had discovered a new trade route to

A religious leader of the Hupa tribe poses for a photograph *(Library of Congress, Prints and Photographs Division [LC-USZ62-115024])*

India. In his journals, Columbus described the "Indians" he encountered (who probably belonged to the Taino tribe) as excellent prospective slaves, and he remarked that "they would easily be made Christians, for they appear to me to have no religion." The false impression that Native Americans have no serious faith traditions of their own continues to this day.

One of the most significant factors contributing to this impression is the fact that American Indian religions are somewhat difficult to study. There is, for example, no single Native American religion; there are as many Native American religions as there are tribes or cultures, and while there is a significant amount of overlap among the tribal religious systems, it is impossible to comprehensively describe American Indian religion "in general." Also significant is the lack of primary source texts. When European nations first began to invade the Americas, all American Indian faiths relied on oral tradition; there were no written scriptures, proverbs, or prayers. For this reason, the only means available to non–Native American scholars to study Native religious traditions was through firsthand observation of religious ceremonies and traditions—a type of contact that is discouraged in many American Indian spiritual traditions, which are usually private and nonevangelical.

Native faiths tend to be strongly nature-centered and focus on practical concerns such as farming, animals, hunting, human life cycles, and healing. Members of American Indian faith traditions tend to identify with their traditions based more on earnest participation in religious ceremonies than on philosophical doctrines about the nature of the universe. Native traditions teach that there is life after death, though spirits of the dead are often described as remaining on earth rather than traveling to an afterlife realm.

Native American religious traditions were once the only faiths represented on the North American continent but since European contact have become a small minority. This is due primarily to immigration—according to the 2000 census, less than 1 percent of the U.S. population now identifies itself as Native American—but it can also be attributed to a number of factors, including large-scale conversion to Christianity. This conversion was sometimes forced by colonial powers and later encouraged by the U.S. federal government, which actively discouraged practice of American Indian religions well into the early 20th century. To accommodate the changing religious beliefs of many Native American Christians while preserving traditional Native American religious ceremonies, some religious organizations—such as the Native American Church—feature syncretic (multireligious) ceremonies that include elements of both religious traditions.

In response to previous oppression of American Indians, the U.S. Congress passed the American Indian Religious Freedom Act (AIRFA) in 1978. This act was mostly symbolic—the freedoms stipulated in the act should have already been protected by the First Amendment—but it did explicitly state that the U.S. government no longer actively sought to eliminate Native American religious traditions. Since that time, most Native American First Amendment controversies have focused on two goals: protection of sacred sites (especially burial sites) and legalized use of peyote, a hallucinogenic drug, during some ceremonies of the Native American Church.

JUDAISM

The first religious Jew to set foot on American soil was probably Joachim Gaunse, a native of Bohemia (in present-day Czech Republic) and member of a 1585 English expedition to Virginia. He was a remarkable figure for several reasons, one being that he was actually welcomed into England by the government. Jews were still officially prohibited from living in England based on a 1290 edict passed after decades of brutal anti-semitic actions (including mass executions) by the government. Gaunse, a mining expert, proved to be such a potentially valuable addition to the team of explorers that the government seemed willing to overlook its immigration policy, at least temporarily. Once he had served his purpose by assisting the expedition, Gaunse returned to England in 1586 and soon faced blasphemy charges for denying the divinity of Jesus. He was to appear in court for sentencing in 1589 but mysteriously vanished from history at that point. There is no known record of the outcome of his trial, or of anything he did afterward, though historians speculate that he was probably smuggled out of the country by sympathetic government officials.

"On and after August 11, 1978, it shall be the policy of the United States to protect and preserve for American Indians their inherent right of freedom to believe, express, and exercise the traditional religions of the American Indian, Eskimo, Aleut, and Native Hawaiians, including but not limited to access to sites, use and possession of sacred objects, and the freedom to worship through ceremonials and traditional rites."

—from the American Indian Religious Freedom Act (1978)

A rabbi teaches a child on Rosh Hashanah, 1907. Rosh Hashanah marks the beginning of each new year on the Jewish lunar calendar. *(Library of Congress, Prints and Photographs Division [LC-USZ62-72466])*

"Happily the government of the United States, which gives to bigotry no sanction, to persecution no assistance, requires only that they who live under its protection should demean themselves as good citizens, in giving it on all occasions their effectual support. . . . May the children of the Stock of Abraham, who dwell in this land, continue to merit and enjoy the good will of the other inhabitants, while every one shall sit in safety under his own vine and fig-tree and there shall be none to make him afraid."

—*President George Washington, in a letter to Touro Synagogue (Newport, Rhode Island), 1790*

At first, the American colonies were only slightly more friendly toward Jewish immigrants. A few individual Jews were able to come over, but when a group of 23 Jews attempted to settle in New Amsterdam (later New York) in 1654, Governor Peter Stuyvesant (1592–1672) wrote a bitterly anti-semitic letter calling on his government to reject the immigrants. Dutch trade authorities overruled Stuyvesant, and although some North American colonies were less willing to admit Jewish immigrants than others (a few even prosecuted Jews for blasphemy—a charge that sometimes carried the death penalty), they gradually abolished anti-semitic laws. By 1790, at least 1,500 religious Jews lived in the United States.

The United States now boasts a Jewish population of more than 6 million—the largest Jewish population on earth, even greater than that of Israel. Judaism is the second-largest religion in America, and next to Christianity, the most well represented in public life. There have been Jewish secretaries of state (Henry Kissinger and Madeleine Albright), Jewish Supreme Court justices (including Louis Brandeis and Felix Frankfurter), and a considerable number of Jewish senators and representatives. Although there has not yet been a Jewish president, it remains a viable future possibility; in 2000, Senator Joseph Lieberman of Connecticut—a devout Orthodox Jew—became the Democratic nominee for vice president. Jews have contributed to every aspect of American life, and the American Jewish population has also played an important role in influencing the global Jewish faith. Two major branches of Judaism (Conservative Judaism and Reconstructionism) originated in the United States, and many of the 19th and 20th centuries' best-known Jewish theologians were Americans. According to a July 2003 poll conducted by the Pew Forum on Religion and Public Life, Judaism is now the most widely respected religion in America: 72 percent of Americans have a favorable opinion of Jews, compared to 70 percent for Christian Protestants and 69 percent for Roman Catholics.

Despite these promising statistics, anti-semitism remains a serious problem in the United States. While popular acceptance of Jews and Judaism is almost universal, a small but vocal minority of anti-Jewish extremists have recently become much more aggressive in their attempts to intimidate Jews through vandalism, arson, death threats, and even occasional cases of assault and murder. In 2002, 1,599 anti-Semitic incidents were reported in the United States—an increase of 8 percent over the previous year. According to a 2002 poll conducted by the Anti-Defamation League (ADL), an estimated 17 percent of Americans hold anti-Semitic beliefs.

In recent decades, the most prominent legal controversy affecting the religious freedom of Jews has dealt with blue laws, city or state ordinances that prohibit businesses from operating on Sundays. Because Jews observe their Sabbath from sundown Friday to sundown Saturday, blue laws essentially require Jewish workers to take two days off—something that many workers cannot afford to do. While the Supreme Court has traditionally held that blue laws are constitutional, such laws have largely vanished and are seldom in effect today.

ISLAM

The first documented case of a Muslim setting foot on American soil is that of Estevanico of Azemmour (1503–39), a Moroccan slave who earned his freedom in the New World. He is responsible for exploring much of what would later become Texas, Arizona, and New Mexico and was a leading expert on Native American languages and customs.

Although a small number of individual Muslims arrived in North America during the 16th and 17th centuries, organized Islam did not emerge in the United States until the late 19th century. The first group of American Muslims was invited into the country during the 1850s to raise camels in the southwestern desert in hopes that the animals might prove to be a viable means of transportation. The experiment was considered a failure, but

The U.S. Muslim population began to expand during the late 19th century. In this photograph from the 1880s, a group of Muslims from around the world gather in Mecca, the international center of Islam, to pray. *(Library of Congress, Prints and Photographs Division [LC-USZ62-99278])*

one of the immigrants—a Syrian Muslim named Hajj Ali (or "Hi Jolly," as he was more commonly called)—became a successful prospector in California.

Early Muslim communities in the United States met in individuals' homes and were not generally large enough to sustain a formal religious community. This was due in part to the strict U.S. immigration laws of the time, which limited or excluded immigration from many predominantly Muslim countries. The first American mosque—the Mother Mosque of America in Cedar Rapids, Iowa—was not built until 1934, and as recently as the 1960s most studies estimated that there were no more than 100,000 Muslims living in the United States. The situation has changed dramatically over the past 40 years as Islam has grown to become America's third-largest religion. There are between 4 and 6 million Muslims living in the United States today, a number that continues to rise every year.

Over the past decade, the number of hate crimes directed against American Muslims has also grown. When the U.S. government first displayed an Islamic star and crescent alongside Christian and Jewish holiday symbols in Washington, D.C., in 1997, vandals tore the star off the display and defaced it with a swastika (a symbol connected with Nazism since the 1930s). The September 11, 2001, terrorist attacks in the United States prompted new waves of violence and harassment against American Muslims, but the long-term effect has not been as profound as many had feared. Although there has been a substantial increase in the number of anti-Muslim incidents since the 9/11 attacks—525 incidents were reported in 2001, 602 were reported in 2002, and 1,019 were reported in 2003—mainstream public acceptance of Islam seems also to have increased since 9/11 as more American non-Muslims have learned about the religion. In a March 2001 poll conducted by the Pew Forum on Religion and Public Life, an estimated 45 percent of Americans described a favorable opinion of American Muslims. When the same poll was conducted again in July 2003, the number had increased to 51 percent.

More than 1,200 Muslims living in the United States as noncitizens (and some who were citizens) were secretly arrested after the 9/11 attacks, and the majority were deported to their home countries. The U.S. Department of Justice has also investigated and shut down dozens of Islamic charities based on little-known links to overseas terrorist organizations. Although President George W. Bush has stated that the Islamic faith is not being targeted and that Muslims are welcome in the United States, the U.S. government's actions have left many American Muslims suspicious and afraid.

THE BLACK MUSLIM MOVEMENT

From the 17th century until the end of the Civil War, American slavery was legal. Enslaved African Americans were kept under control by a number of threats and practices, ranging from sale, torture, or increased labor to execution. It has been argued that one of the most effective tools was a popular 19th-century proslavery interpretation of Christianity, which commanded slaves to "count their own masters worthy of all honour" and "do them service, because they are faithful and beloved" (1 Timothy 6:1–2). According to proslavery theology, an obedient, submissive slave could count on being rewarded in the afterlife. When slavery was abolished, the Ku Klux Klan (KKK) was founded as an organization of "Christian" intimidators. Its members used the burning cross to frighten and perceived it as a Christian symbol. In the 20th century, when the civil rights movement drew strength from powerful Christian leaders such as Martin Luther King, Jr., white supremacists railed from the pulpits declaring all African Americans to be the cursed descendants of Ham (Genesis 9:25), forever condemned to torment and degradation. Even today, many white supremacist organizations couch their rhetoric in biblical language.

These factors, coupled with some of Islam's natural strengths, have led millions of African-American Christians to Islam. Islam relies less on institutional and communal power structures than most forms of Christianity do, emphasizing instead an individual relationship with God and a passionate, voluntary identification with fellow Muslims. Unlike American Christianity, Islam's tradition is not as interwoven with that of the U.S. government, which has a history of discrimination against African Americans. At the same time, it is a global spiritual movement with a rich history, strong moral values, and a compelling tradition of worship.

HINDUISM AND BUDDHISM

The presence of Asian religions in the United States has been determined largely by U.S. immigration policy. Until the mid-1960s, Asian immigrants represented a tiny minority of overall U.S. immigrants; in the past decades, the number of Asian Americans has

There have been some movements within Islam dedicated specifically to African Americans. The best known is the Nation of Islam (NOI), founded by Wali D. Fard (1891–1934) in 1930, which achieved its peak during the 1960s under the leadership of Elijah Muhammad (1897–1975). NOI theology was very unconventional, holding that Wali D. Fard was God incarnate and Elijah Muhammad the reincarnation of the prophet Muhammad (two beliefs that many orthodox Muslims found offensive) and that whites are an inferior race of devils created by black scientists during an ancient experiment. When Elijah Muhammad died in 1975, the group underwent a schism, prompted in part by the death a decade earlier of the influential and popular NOI leader and civil rights activist Malcolm X (1925–65), who had converted to a more traditional form of Islam and was murdered by three members of the NOI shortly thereafter.

The American Muslim Mission, led by Elijah Muhammad's son Warith Deen Muhammad, proposes a traditional Sunni Muslim philosophy and has abandoned the more unorthodox beliefs of the NOI. Meanwhile, the Nation of Islam as it exists today is led by Louis Farrakhan and has sponsored a number of highly visible events such as the Million Man March of 1995. The NOI represents a minority of African-American Muslims (most of whom belong to more orthodox Muslim traditions) but remains an influential force in American public life.

Today, about 30 percent of American Muslims (roughly 2 million people) and an estimated two-thirds of American converts to Islam are African American. African-American Muslims play a major role in traditional Islam as it is represented in the United States, and most American Muslim celebrities (such as Muhammad Ali and Kareem Abdul-Jabbar) are African American.

increased and, with it, the number of Americans who belong to Asian faiths.

Very few Asian Indians lived in the United States until the first year of the 20th century, when an estimated 7,000 Punjabi workers who had helped to construct the Canadian railroad system came to the United States. As more Indians immigrated to the

United States, they faced a mixed welcome. A small but influential organization called the Asian Exclusion League (AEL) worked to prohibit Indian immigration to the United States by exploiting the fear that Indians were stealing "American" jobs. In 1907 the AEL successfully instigated a major riot in the city of Bellingham, Washington, which was home to more than 400 Indians at the time. The police did nothing to prevent the rioters, arrested the city's entire Indian population, and expelled them en masse, just as the AEL and rioters had demanded. The AEL was also successful in achieving its goals through legislative means, such as supporting a California law prohibiting all noncitizens from owning land.

Immigration laws of the time officially prevented nonwhite persons from becoming American citizens, but Indians were originally exempt from this restriction under the precedent set by *United States v. Balsara* (1910), in which the U.S. Supreme Court declared Indians to be white. When the need for railroad labor decreased and racist prejudice against Asians became more predominant, the Court took an unusual step in *United States v. Thind* (1923) by reversing its previous decision and retroactively stripping Indian immigrants of their U.S. citizenship. Thousands of Indian Americans either fled the country or were forced out, leaving only 2,405 Indians in the United States at the beginning of World War II (1939–45).

Because documents of the time described Indians of all faiths as "Hindus," it is impossible to know how many actually belonged to the Hindu religion. Most historians believe that the earliest Indian immigrants were probably Christian converts, and public expression of the Hindu faith was extremely scarce. Hindus generally practiced their faith alone or in small groups, and the first traditional Hindu temple in North America—the Sri Maha Vallabha Ganapati Devasthanam in Flushing, New York—did not open until 1977.

Buddhism was better represented during the 18th and 19th centuries, primarily because of a large 19th-century Chinese immigrant population. The first U.S. Buddhist temple, the Tien Hau Temple of San Francisco, opened in 1852 and would become one of hundreds of Buddhist temples scattered throughout the U.S. West Coast. In 1880, almost 20 years before the first large-scale arrival of

Indian immigrants, more than 30,000 Chinese Americans had already made their home in the United States. Like Indians, however, they met with discrimination. The Los Angeles Chinese Massacre of 1871 was similar in effect to the Bellingham riots, but it was both earlier and bloodier: 19 Chinese Americans were killed, and thousands more were driven out of the city. Chinese Americans would later be prohibited from testifying in court, excluded from the public school system, and formally prevented from immigrating to the United States or becoming U.S. citizens through the Chinese Exclusion Act of 1882. A small number of Japanese immigrants, who also brought Buddhism to the United States, faced similar restrictions by late 19th-century exclusion laws.

Because the Asian-American population was relatively small until the mid-1960s, and Asian Americans were generally excluded from many aspects of public life, most Americans familiar with Hinduism or Buddhism had learned about the traditions from non-Asian thinkers. British translators had produced excellent English editions of classical Hindu and Buddhist texts, and influential 19th-century American writers such as Ralph Waldo Emerson (1803–82) and Henry David Thoreau (1817–62) had grown enthralled with what they were able to learn of the Hindu and Buddhist faiths. Public attention to the traditions increased further due to Chicago's 1893 World Parliament of Religions, in which articulate defenders of the Asian faiths such as the Hindu mystic Swami Vivekananda (1863–1902) and Buddhist philosopher Anagarika Dharmapala (1864–1933) visited the United States to present compelling firsthand descriptions of what their faiths were like in practice, drawing a substantial number of influential American disciples.

Despite this interest, people who had been raised in predominantly Hindu or Buddhist countries still had great difficulty immigrating to the United States. The Immigration Act of 1924 made matters even more difficult by in effect freezing all large-scale Asian immigration for 40 years; although the United States began allowing some immigration from Asian countries during the latter years of World War II, strict quotas were enforced to prevent significant growth in the Asian-American population. The McCarran-Walter Act of 1952 allowed for only 2,990 Asian immigrants per year, compared to 149,667 European immigrants. The

"In the morning I bathe my intellect in the stupendous and cosmogonal philosophy of the *Bhagavad-Gita*, since whose composition years of the gods have elapsed, and in comparison with which our modern world and its literature seems puny and trivial."

—*Henry David Thoreau,* Walden *(1854)*

THE WORLD PARLIAMENT OF RELIGIONS

During the 19th century, Asian Americans represented less than 1 percent of the U.S. population. Those who adhered to traditional Asian religions, such as Hinduism or Buddhism, generally practiced their faiths privately, and most U.S. citizens had never been confronted with native-born missionaries representing these traditions.

This began to change in 1893 at the World Parliament of Religions, which was at the time one of the most widely anticipated cultural events in the United States. Held in Chicago, it introduced American audiences and readers to three brilliant advocates for Asian religion: Swami Vivekananda (representing Hinduism), Anagarika Dharmapala (representing Theravada Buddhism), and Shaku Soyen (representing Zen Buddhism).

Born Narendranath Datta, Swami Vivekananda was a Hindu monk following the tradition of Sri Ramakrishna, who advocated Advaita Vedanta, a particular form of Hindu philosophy that proposes God is the only true reality and enlightenment consists of fully recognizing one's own identity as a manifestation of God. The quick-witted but respectful Vivekananda gave what is generally remembered as the most impressive speech at the parliament, prompting one observer to remark, "That man a heathen—and we send missionaries to this people! It would be more fitting that they send missionaries to us." Vivekananda filled that role in many respects, spending four years in the United States lecturing on Hinduism and attracting a substantial number of American converts.

Anagarika Dharmapala, a Sri Lankan Buddhist, was born David Hewavitharana; he changed his name in protest of the Westernized names that Sri Lankans living under British rule often assigned their children. With an extensive background in both Buddhism and secular science, Dharmapala was the first native Theravada Buddhist scholar to lecture in the United States and was highly sought after as a speaker, though he was sometimes baffled by the expectation many Americans had for instant, dramatic religious experiences.

Shaku Soyen (1859–1919), a Japanese Zen Buddhist monk, also became a popular and influential speaker in the United States. Even more influential, however, was one of his pupils, Daisetz T. Suzuki (1869–1966), who became the 20th century's most well-known and widely respected guide to traditional Zen Buddhism. Suzuki's many books on Buddhism are still widely read today.

Until the World Parliament of Religions, most European Americans who had any familiarity with Hinduism or Buddhism judged them almost entirely by their scriptures. The parliament introduced American thinkers to these faiths as they were actually lived, reminding American students of Hinduism and Buddhism of their human side. It was also the first large-scale conference ever brought together for the specific purpose of public discussion among representatives of all major world religions, establishing a tradition of interreligious dialogue that continues to this day.

A group of Japanese-American Buddhists leave a religious service at Manzanar Relocation Center in California. After the United States entered World War II against the Axis powers (Germany, Italy, and Japan), 120,000 Japanese Americans—most of them citizens of the United States—were forcibly imprisoned in Manzanar and other internment camps without trial. *(Library of Congress, Prints and Photographs Division [LC-A35-T01-6-M-34])*

objective was clear: Those supporting the legislation did not want to shift the U.S. ethnic balance by letting a large number of non-whites into the country.

The civil rights movement of the 1960s brought about criticism of racism in general, and the attention of lawmakers soon turned to immigration policies. The revolutionary Immigration Act of 1965 greatly increased the U.S. Asian-American population by allowing admittance of up to 170,000 Asian immigrants per year. Since that time, Hindu and Buddhist influence on the United States has increased dramatically—and, with an open immigration policy still in effect, will probably continue to increase in the years ahead as more Asians from predominantly Hindu and Buddhist countries contribute to the American religious landscape.

Buddhism is now the fourth-largest religion in the United States. The U.S. Buddhist population has been estimated at roughly 3 million and is still growing rapidly by means of both immigration and conversion. Buddhist meditation practices have also become

"Today, in this great hall, are assembled the elected representatives of the people of this nation. They are ready to perform their duties. God, please guide them in their thoughts and actions so they can achieve the greatest good for all."

—Sri Venkatachalapathi Samuldrala, from his prayer in the U.S. Congress, September 14, 2000

popular religious exercises among non-Buddhists and have had a profound influence on Christian and Jewish contemplative prayer practices. Likewise, Hinduism has increased in size to become the fifth-largest religion in the United States with an estimated 1.4 million adherents. Its increasingly credible position in public life was made clear on September 14, 2000, when Hindu priest Venkatachalapathi Samuldrala led the U.S. Congress in its traditional morning prayer.

In addition to Hinduism and Buddhism, other religious communities dedicated to the Asian faiths of Sikhism, Jainism, and Shinto have become more prominent in American life. Every religion popular in Asia—or, indeed, anywhere else on earth—is represented in the United States.

AMERICAN RELIGIOUS PLURALISM TODAY

U.S. religious culture has become increasingly diverse, and reactions to that diversity have been mixed. Some feel that the United States is a historically Christian nation and that the U.S. emphasis on individual rights and democracy will not be possible if it loses its predominantly Christian cultural identity. Others argue that religious diversity represents an evolutionary step in the United States's development as a democratic and multicultural nation and that opposition to non-Christian religious movements violates every principle central to American democracy.

As minority faith communities build roots and gain strength in U.S. culture, religious diversity will no doubt become even more of an obvious reality than it is now—and political opposition to that diversity seems to be waning. National political figures once spoke of "churches," then of "churches and synagogues," and now of "churches, synagogues, and mosques." Religious conservatives who once spoke of encoding Christian principles in government now speak of faith-based initiatives that accommodate every faith tradition equally. Perhaps most important of all, American members of minority faiths are taking on a more prominent role in public life and have become more visible in popular culture. Whether one opposes religious diversity or relishes it, one fact is clear: It is here to stay.

4

Religious Expression and the Law

Although the First Amendment's protection of religious expression has been less widely disputed than its ban on government establishment of religion, the interpretation of what has been called the "free exercise clause" has not been entirely without controversy. The U.S. Supreme Court has attempted to balance consistent enforcement of laws with the constitutional restriction on laws "prohibiting the free exercise [of religion]," which is extraordinarily difficult to achieve given the diverse forms of religious expression and the necessity of protecting public order.

ESTABLISHING THE BOUNDARIES OF FREE EXERCISE

The first free exercise clause case to reach the U.S. Supreme Court was *Reynolds v. United States* (1879), which challenged the constitutionality of the Morrill Act of 1862. The Morrill Act was passed by Congress primarily as a restriction on the Church of Jesus Christ of Latter-day Saints (the Mormons), a growing Christian denomination that settled in territory they named Deseret (now known as Utah) in 1847 after their founder, Joseph Smith (1805–44), was lynched in Illinois. Early Mormons held some doctrines that were regarded as strange by most Roman Catholic and Protestant standards, the most controversial being the belief that polygamy (a man having more than one wife) was natural and worth encouraging. The Morrill Act criminalized polygamy but remained unenforced, partly due to the fact that virtually all state judges in the

PERSECUTION OF THE MORMONS

The Church of Jesus Christ of Latter-day Saints formed in 1830 upon the publication of the *Book of Mormon,* a collection of scriptures that founder Joseph Smith believed to be the word of God as revealed to him. According to Smith, a group of Israelites had traveled to North America sometime near 600 B.C., founded a Jewish civilization, and were visited by Jesus Christ.

The Mormons settled Independence in Jackson County, Missouri, in 1831. Their practice of polygamy, unusual religious beliefs, growing political power, and financial success frustrated some in neighboring communities, and violent riots in 1833 and 1834 forced the Mormons north to Clay County. To address the conflict, the Missouri state legislature created a new Mormon county called Far West, where one-third of the state's Mormon population gathered—the rest remaining in other counties. When state legislator William Peniston

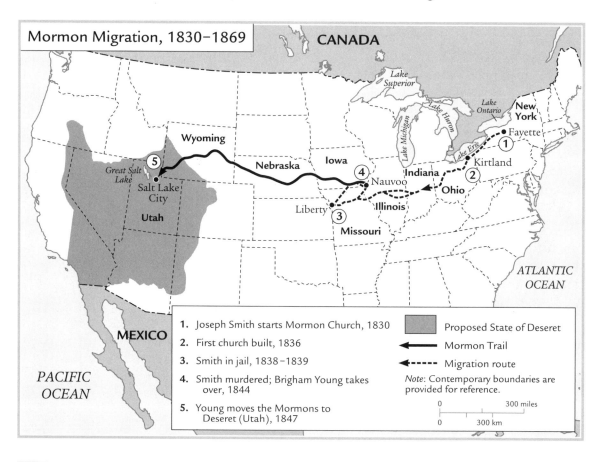

Mormon Migration, 1830–1869

CANADA

Lake Superior

Lake Ontario

New York

Fayette

Wyoming

Nebraska   Iowa

Indiana   Kirtland

Great Salt Lake

Salt Lake City

Nauvoo   Ohio

Utah

Liberty   Illinois

Missouri

PACIFIC OCEAN

MEXICO

ATLANTIC OCEAN

1. Joseph Smith starts Mormon Church, 1830
2. First church built, 1836
3. Smith in jail, 1838–1839
4. Smith murdered; Brigham Young takes over, 1844
5. Young moves the Mormons to Deseret (Utah), 1847

Proposed State of Deseret

Mormon Trail

Migration route

Note: Contemporary boundaries are provided for reference.

0   300 miles

0   300 km

stood to lose an election in August 1838 due to the Mormon vote, he called on local townsfolk to forcibly prevent Mormons from showing up at the polls and, when he lost anyway, falsely claimed that hundreds of Mormons had organized to threaten the lives of non-Mormons. The situation escalated further when a state militia leader arrested three Mormons and faced an angry crowd of Mormon militia members who attempted to release them. To address this purported menace, Missouri governor Lilburn W. Boggs passed the Mormon Extermination Order of 1838, which stated that "Mormons must be treated as enemies and must be exterminated or driven from the state, if necessary for the public good." An angry mob descended on Far West, attacking countless Mormons, destroying their property, and killing dozens (including children and the elderly). Mormons were prohibited from planting crops over the winter, resulting in mass starvation, and faced death if they did not leave the state by February 1839.

The Mormons fared little better when they fled to Illinois and founded the town of Nauvoo under the leadership of Smith. Nearby residents clashed with Mormons in a series of violent riots called the Mormon War, which ultimately resulted in the death of Smith, murdered by an angry mob in his jail cell after being arrested on riot charges. By the end of 1846, the Mormons began their long pilgrimage to what was then the unsettled Mexican territory of Utah, where they founded the first American colony in July 1847. The state became a U.S. territory early the next year, and Mormons lived in relative peace for several decades.

After the Morrill Act and the *Reynolds* decision, the U.S. Congress passed a number of other laws designed to prevent polygamy, reduce the political influence of Mormons, and assimilate them into mainstream American culture. The Edmunds Act of 1882, banning "unlawful cohabitation," was specifically written to allow federal judges to prosecute Mormons on polygamy charges without actually proving that a wedding had ever taken place. Although most Mormons did not practice polygamy, the fact that some Mormons did—and that it was permitted under the law of the church—inspired hostility from lawmakers. Idaho revoked all Mormons' citizenship rights in 1883, as the First Amendment had not yet been applied to state law. In 1887, the U.S. Congress's Edmunds-Tucker Act took matters even further: It confiscated all Latter-day Saints church property not actually used for worship or burial; prohibited women from voting, as the Utah Territory allowed women's suffrage, which, it was supposed, gave extra political power to families practicing polygamy; and forced all prospective voters to swear an oath against polygamy. The Church of Jesus Christ of Latter-day Saints relented in 1890 by banning polygamy among its members and has faced relatively little government persecution since.

A member of the Church of Jesus Christ of Latter-day Saints with his six wives. During the 19th century, a small percentage of Mormons openly practiced polygamy. *(Library of Congress, Prints and Photographs Division [LC-USZ62-83877])*

Utah Territory were Mormons sympathetic to the practice of polygamy and also partly due to the fact that Mormon temple weddings were private, making it difficult to prove that a marriage had actually taken place. As non-Mormon immigration to Utah increased after the Civil War, the U.S. Congress passed the Poland Law in 1874, giving federal judges jurisdiction over Utah's polygamy cases.

The first man arrested under the Morrill Act was George Reynolds, a prominent Mormon author and religious leader who had been turned in by one of his wives. Reynolds appealed his case before the Supreme Court on the grounds that the Morrill Act violated the free exercise clause of the First Amendment. In a unanimous verdict, the Supreme Court ruled against Reynolds and held that the Morrill Act was constitutional.

In his ruling, Chief Justice Morrison Waite (1816–88) argued that the free exercise clause protects only religious belief, not religious practice. Any religious practice—even worship—could be restricted by law under the *Reynolds* standard, especially if it "is in violation of social duties or subversive of good order." Although the word *exercise* explicitly specifies religious practice, First Amendment law was a new and unrefined concept in 1879. It had no history, no established norms, and very little weight, as the Supreme Court had never overturned any legislation on First Amendment grounds. The importance of the *Reynolds* case is that it established a line of judicial reasoning on the issue of religious expression—a line of reasoning that would evolve dramatically over time. In the years since the *Reynolds* decision, the U.S. Supreme Court has alternated between two readings of the free exercise clause: the nondiscrimination interpretation and the preferred freedoms interpretation.

TWO SCHOOLS OF THOUGHT

According to the nondiscrimination interpretation of the First Amendment, the ban on "laws prohibiting the free exercise [of religion]" refers only to laws whose purpose is to restrict a religious tradition or religious practice, regardless of the laws' secondary effects. It is called the nondiscrimination interpretation because it affirms the validity of any law that has a secular purpose and does not discriminate against religious practices. Laws neutral to religion are not affected by the free exercise clause under this interpretation regardless of what their effects may be, and they need not meet any special standards to survive a constitutional challenge. According to the nondiscrimination interpretation, the *Reynolds* ruling was flawed, but the verdict itself was correct.

The preferred freedoms interpretation holds that the free exercise clause should be taken into account when dealing with any law where its effect restricts a religious tradition or religious practice, even if the law has a legitimate secular purpose. It is called the preferred freedoms interpretation because it holds that the freedoms guaranteed by the First Amendment are in a preferred position and that the Constitution gives them special protection. Any law that restricts religious practice—whether it is neutral to religion or not—must serve a "compelling interest" in order to survive a constitutional challenge. The preferred freedoms interpretation would not protect ceremonial house burglaries, because preventing burglaries

"[H]ere, as a law of the organization of society under the exclusive dominion of the United States, it is provided that plural marriages shall not be allowed. Can a man excuse his practices to the contrary because of his religious belief? To permit this would be to make the professed doctrines of religious belief superior to the law of the land, and in effect to permit every citizen to become a law unto himself. Government could exist only in name under such circumstances."

—*Chief Justice Morrison Waite of the Supreme Court, from his majority ruling in* Reynolds v. United States *(1879)*

would be seen as a satisfactory compelling interest. On the other hand, the preferred freedoms interpretation could be a challenge to *Reynolds;* those defending the Morrill Act would have to prove that a ban on polygamy is important enough to justify restricting a religious practice.

The nondiscrimination interpretation has been criticized on the grounds that it does not protect religious liberty enough, while the preferred freedoms interpretation has been criticized on the grounds that it is vague and gives too much power to the courts. Both positions, however, allow more room for free religious exercise than *Reynolds,* which would have implicitly given the government almost unlimited power to restrict religious practices provided that it did not restrict religious beliefs.

For 60 years, the Supreme Court faced no major cases explicitly dealing with the religion clause of the First Amendment (though some had religious implications). This was primarily because the Supreme Court did not establish that the Bill of Rights had jurisdiction over state law until 1925 and because there were relatively few federal laws dealing with religion. It was not until the case of *Cantwell v. Connecticut* (1940) that the Supreme Court extended the First Amendment's religion clauses to the states.

THE SUPREME COURT DEBATES FREE EXERCISE

Newton Cantwell belonged to the Jehovah's Witnesses, an evangelical Christian denomination that originated in the United States. The Jehovah's Witnesses tradition places great emphasis on distribution of religious literature, regarded by its adherents as a necessary means of evangelism, and also encourages subjects of its missionary activities to purchase books about the Jehovah's Witnesses tradition. When Cantwell was arrested by the state of Connecticut for "soliciting" without a license, he appealed his case to the Supreme Court. In a unanimous ruling written by Justice Owen J. Roberts, the Court held that "a State may not, by statute, wholly deny the right to preach or to disseminate religious views" and overturned Cantwell's conviction.

At roughly the same time, Jehovah's Witnesses in several states were arrested on the more specific charge of selling books without a license. In the case referred to as *Jones v. the City of Opelika I* (1942), the Supreme Court held that such distribution of books and pamphlets could be restricted by law because a secular interest was being met and because the sale of books, whatever role religion might play in that enterprise, was intrinsically commercial, not religious. Writing for the slim 5-4 majority, Justice Stanley Reed (1884–1980) argued that "[t]o subject any religious or didactic group to a reasonable fee for their money-making activities does not require a finding that the licensed acts are purely commercial." In his dissenting opinion, Justice Frank Murphy (1890–1949) disagreed on the grounds that the Jehovah's Witnesses sale of books and pamphlets was more religious than commercial; without asking for donations, the Jehovah's Witnesses would be unable to afford the fees required to publish their pamphlets and would therefore be prohibited from "spread[ing] the Gospel as they understand it."

"The way of the religious dissenter has long been hard. But if the formula of this type of ordinance is approved, a new device for the suppression of religious minorities will have been found. . . . The spread of religious ideas through personal visitations by the literature ministry of numerous religious groups would be stopped. The fact that the ordinance is 'nondiscriminatory' is immaterial. The protection afforded by the First Amendment is not so restricted. A license tax does not acquire constitutional validity because it classifies the privileges protected by the First Amendment along with the wares and merchandise of hucksters and peddlers and treats them all alike. . . . Freedom of press, freedom of speech, freedom of religion are in a preferred position."

—*Supreme Court justice William O. Douglas, from his majority ruling in* Jones v. City of Opelika II *(1943)*

With the retirement of Justice James Francis Byrnes (1879–1972) and the appointment of Justice Wiley Blount Rutledge (1894–1949), the Supreme Court's 5-4 majority came to favor Murphy's interpretation in a similar case, *Murdock v. Pennsylvania* (1943). Because it had come to a different conclusion on the issue, the Court ordered a rehearing of *Jones v. Opelika*. In the case generally referred to as *Jones v. City of Opelika II* (1943), the Court overturned the original verdict and affirmed the Jehovah's Witnesses' right to distribute pamphlets while asking for donations. "Those who can tax the exercise of this religious practice," argued Justice William O. Douglas (1898–1980) in his majority opinion, "can make its exercise so costly as to deprive it of the resources necessary for its maintenance."

The second *Jones* case is considered extremely important to the history of the free exercise clause because it affirmed the preferred freedoms interpretation over the nondiscrimination interpretation. A nondiscriminatory law prohibiting unlicensed book sales was overturned by the Supreme Court on the grounds that it restricted

RELIGIOUS ATTIRE IN THE MILITARY

Like many Orthodox Jewish rabbis, Dr. S. Simcha Goldman wore a yarmulke (skullcap) to work. Goldman, however, was a captain in the U.S. Air Force, where he served as a clinical psychologist. Although air force Regulation 35-10 states that "[h]eadgear will not be worn . . . while indoors except by armed security police," he wore his yarmulke indoors for years without receiving any formal complaints. It was not until he testified as a witness in a court-martial hearing that his right to wear a yarmulke was challenged; the opposing counsel filed a complaint arguing that his decision to wear a yarmulke indoors violated air force regulations, and his base commander asked him to remove it. To avoid a court martial, Goldman challenged the U.S. Air Force's policy on the grounds that it violated the free exercise clause. After separate rulings both favoring and rejecting his argument, Goldman's case was appealed to the Supreme Court.

In *Goldman v. Weinberger* (1986), the Supreme Court held—by only 5-4 margin—that the air force's policy did not violate the free exercise clause. Writing for the majority, Justice William H. Rehnquist (1924–) argued that the military was a "specialized society" in which uniformity of dress served a functional purpose. The verdict was considered highly controversial at the time, so much so that Equal Employment Opportunity Commission chairman and future Supreme Court justice Clarence Thomas issued a policy memo reassuring concerned

Americans that the ruling only applied to the military and that preventing employees from wearing religious attire in the workplace would still be regarded as discriminatory and prosecuted appropriately. In 1987, the U.S. Congress revised the military codes to allow those serving in the military to wear yarmulkes or other "neat and conservative" religious apparel.

An Orthodox Jewish army chaplain serving in World War II. During the 1980s, the wearing of the yarmulke (skullcap) by Jewish military chaplains became a controversial First Amendment issue. *(Library of Congress, Prints and Photographs Division [LC-USW3-001749-D])*

free religious exercise, even though its purpose was not religious and even though it served a legitimate secular purpose. Over the next 20 years the preferred freedoms interpretation slowly became the Supreme Court's most frequently used reading of the free exercise clause, reaching its peak in the case of *Sherbert v. Verner* (1963).

Adelle Sherbert belonged to the Seventh-Day Adventists, a Christian denomination that celebrates its Sabbath on Saturday. After being fired from a clothing factory for refusing to work on Saturdays and finding no job that did not require her to do so, Sherbert filed for unemployment benefits and was rejected on the grounds that she had "failed, without good cause, to accept available suitable work when offered." She challenged the decision before the Supreme Court, which ruled in her favor. In his majority ruling, Justice William J. Brennan (1906–97) wrote, "Only the gravest abuses, endangering paramount interests, give occasion for permissible limitation [on religious freedom]." Any secular law that restricted religious freedom could now be challenged under this strict precedent. The preferred freedoms interpretation had triumphed.

> "We have never held that an individual's religious beliefs excuse him from compliance with an otherwise valid law prohibiting conduct that the State is free to regulate. . . . To make an individual's obligation to obey such a law contingent upon the law's coincidence with his religious beliefs, except where the State's interest is 'compelling' . . . contradicts both constitutional tradition and common sense. . . . [W]e cannot afford the luxury of deeming presumptively invalid . . . every regulation of conduct that does not protect an interest of the highest order."
>
> —*Supreme Court justice Antonin Scalia, from his majority ruling in* Employment Division v. Smith *(1990)*

THE RETURN OF THE NONDISCRIMINATION INTERPRETATION

For 27 years, the preferred freedoms interpretation of the free exercise clause was essentially the law of the land. General laws of a secular purpose that interfered with religious liberty had to serve a "compelling interest" in order to survive a constitutional challenge.

This unexpectedly changed in *Employment Division v. Smith* (1990). Alfred Smith and Galen Black worked as counselors in a drug and alcohol rehabilitation center but were fired after using a small amount of peyote—a hallucinogenic drug, which was illegal at that time—as part of a Native American religious ceremony.

"Because the First Amendment does not distinguish between religious belief and religious conduct, conduct motivated by sincere religious belief, like the belief itself, must be at least presumptively protected by the free exercise clause. . . . The compelling interest test reflects the First Amendment's mandate of preserving religious liberty to the fullest extent possible in a pluralistic society. For the Court to deem this command a 'luxury' is to denigrate the very purpose of a Bill of Rights."

—Supreme Court justice Sandra Day O'Connor, from her opinion in Employment Division v. Smith *(1990)*

When they applied for unemployment benefits, they were turned down on the grounds that their use of peyote constituted a "work-related misconduct."

The 5-3 verdict against Smith and Black was not surprising; many legal scholars expected the Supreme Court to rule that the regulation of illegal drugs constituted a compelling interest. What Justice Antonin Scalia (1936–   ) did in his majority ruling, however, was rule that the compelling interest standard no longer needed to be met at all. In his ruling, the Court explicitly returned to the nondiscrimination interpretation. "[I]f prohibiting the free exercise of religion [is] merely the incidental effect of a generally applicable and otherwise valid provision," Scalia wrote, "the First Amendment has not been offended." This meant that laws with a secular purpose did not have to meet any special standards to justify restricting religious freedom. Justice Sandra Day O'Connor (1930–   ) wrote a separate opinion ruling against Smith and Black using the compelling interest standard, but she represented a minority of justices, and the philosophy of the Court on the free exercise clause was clear. The preferred freedoms interpretation had been shelved, at least temporarily, in favor of the nondiscrimination standard.

The Supreme Court's return to the nondiscrimination standard provoked widespread outrage. "[U]nder the Court's view of the First Amendment," wrote one journalist in *National Catholic Reporter,* "a neutral and generally applicable criminal law that prohibited the consumption of alcohol could be enforced against a Catholic priest and the communicants who drank wine during the Eucharist." Congress responded with the Religious Freedom Restoration Act (RFRA) of 1993.

The RFRA specified that the government could restrict religious liberty only in cases where it "(1) is essential to further a compelling governmental interest; and (2) is the least restrictive means of furthering that compelling government interest." The RFRA, in other words, was an attempt to enforce the preferred freedoms interpretation by passing a law. The bill received unprecedented widespread support. It was endorsed by both the American Civil Liberties Union (ACLU) and the Family Research Council (FRC), two organizations that are almost always opposed to each other. It also brought together liberal legislators such as Massachusetts senator Edward Kennedy and conservative legislators such as South Carolina senator Jesse Helms to pass the act by an astounding 97-3 margin in the Senate. Both liberals and conservatives angrily opposed the *Smith* ruling for roughly the same reason: They felt that it weakened the free exercise clause.

When the RFRA was struck down by the Supreme Court in a 1997 ruling, few were surprised. The RFRA was a law passed by the U.S. Congress dictating the behavior of the U.S. Supreme Court, an equal branch of government, and the U.S. Congress was no more empowered to order the Supreme Court to render a verdict than the Supreme Court would have been empowered to order the U.S. Congress to pass a law. The main benefit of the RFRA was its symbolic value; it was a way of showing, in impressive terms, that the *Smith* decision would not be accepted without controversy.

Although the nondiscrimination interpretation is extremely unpopular, it still protects religious practices under most circumstances. In *Church of Lukumi Babalu Aye v. City of Hileah* (1993), for example, the Court struck down a Florida city statute barring animal sacrifices on the grounds that it was discriminatory, written to restrict the religious practices of Santería (a religion developed in the Caribbean based on West African beliefs, which had recently begun to emerge in Florida).

Over a period of 125 years, the Supreme Court has shifted from implicit approval of laws restricting religious practice to the current debate, which deals with the question of how religious practices can be best protected. Whether the Supreme Court will return to the preferred freedoms interpretation in the coming decades—or adopt a completely new standard—remains to be seen.

"We seem to have forgotten that the very first sentence of the first amendment to the Constitution guarantees not freedom of speech or assembly, or even freedom of the press. The first freedom of our Bill of Rights is the freedom of religious expression. . . . These words—direct, but all too often misunderstood— were not designed to protect a defenseless government from the encroachments of religion, but rather to protect religion from an overreaching government."

—*Republican senator Bob Dole of Kansas, Senate speech in support of the Religious Freedom Restoration Act of 1993, October 27, 1993*

5

Conscientious Objectors and the Draft

Although the term *conscientious objector* technically applies to anyone who objects to something as a matter of conscience, it is nearly always used to describe citizens who are drafted but refuse to serve in the military due to deep-seated moral or religious concerns. From Quaker "non-resisters" of 17th-century Massachusetts to secular humanist pacifists of the 1960s, conscientious objectors have consistently played a significant role in U.S. draft policy.

Conscientious objection has faded from public life since the draft was canceled at the conclusion of the Vietnam War, but the draft's framework—the Selective Service System—has remained in effect. If the U.S. draft is ever reinstated, conscientious objection will once again become a sensitive, hotly debated issue.

THE BIRTH OF CONSCIENTIOUS OBJECTION IN AMERICA

In addition to being the first organized group of American conscientious objectors, the Quakers were the most prominent and outspoken. Their refusal to bear arms in combat against American Indians earned them the disapproval of many of their fellow colonists, and some colonial governments began levying fines against Quakers for refusing to bear arms, fines that the most stringent Quakers were bound not to pay (as the fines, which functioned as a means of buying off military service, financially supported the very conflicts that Quakers opposed).

Over time, some colonial governments grew more sympathetic to the concerns of conscientious objectors and passed resolutions formally exempting them from military service. One of the first was the Puritan colony of Massachusetts, which in 1661 allowed "non-resisters" to avoid bearing arms. The religiously tolerant state of Rhode Island and the Quaker state of Pennsylvania also included conscientious objector clauses as part of their state constitutions. By the end of the 17th century, conscientious objection had become, if not a popular idea, at least a somewhat common one. The Quakers were not the only group of organized conscientious objectors, having been joined by the Mennonites, some Brethren sects, and individual adherents of more mainstream denominations who had come to see war as evil.

The atmosphere changed dramatically during the 18th century, particularly during the American Revolution (1775–83). Because the Revolution consisted of a group of individual American citizens uniting to take up arms against a professional army sent over by the British, those not participating in the war were seen by many as nonparticipants in the revolutionary cause. Even Pennsylvania—a state founded on Quaker principles—established draft laws shortly after the war began. Although it was often possible to avoid military service by paying fines or hiring substitutes, these were not possible options for the most strict conscientious objectors—and neither was payment of the "war tax," used to support the war effort. Accusations of cowardice and British loyalism haunted many strict American pacifists, who were often punished with fines, imprisonment, and open hostility.

After the war, some American political thinkers sought to protect at least the more moderate conscientious objectors in some sort of definitive way. In his original proposal for a Bill of Rights, James Madison suggested a Second Amendment that both protected "[t]he right of the people to keep and bear arms" and established that "no person religiously scrupulous of bearing arms shall be compelled to render military service in person." The latter clause was removed by Congress during debate, effectively striking down conscientious objection as an explicit constitutional right. Since that time conscientious objector status has been determined on the basis of existing draft laws, though many believe that it is implicitly protected by the First Amendment's ban on legislation "prohibiting the free exercise [of religion]."

CONSCIENTIOUS OBJECTION DURING THE NINETEENTH CENTURY

By the start of the 19th century, the United States was an independent country, the draft had been abolished, and the remaining military was made up of willing volunteers. Both conscientious objectors and entrepreneurs turned their attention away from war and toward peacetime pursuits.

The possibility of reviving the draft (military conscription) came up during the War of 1812 (1812–14), in which the U.S. Army was once more engaged in war against British forces and found itself in need of more soldiers. President James Madison supported a new measure that would draft civilians into the military, much as had been the case prior to the end of the Revolution. Conscientious objectors opposed the war once again, and this time were joined by a large number of libertarians led by the charismatic senator Daniel Webster (1782–1852), who felt that the draft was an unconstitutional relic incompatible with American democracy. The draft was defeated, and it would be another half century before its return.

No longer forced to focus on keeping its members out of war, the Quakers and other pacifist churches instead turned their attention to what would become the most divisive issue of the time: slavery. In the years leading up to the Civil War, many pacifist churches focused on abolishing slavery, and many other slavery opponents took a second, critical look at the prospect of ever waging war on behalf of a government that promoted it.

When the Civil War first broke out, in 1861, the Union government portrayed the war as being completely neutral to slavery. "If I could save the Union without freeing any slave," stated President Abraham Lincoln in March 1862, "I would do it; and if I could save it by freeing all the slaves, I would do it; and if I could save it by freeing some and leaving

"The nation is not yet in a temper to submit to conscription. The people have too fresh and strong a feeling of the blessings of civil liberty to be willing thus to surrender them. . . . A military force cannot be raised, in this manner, but by the means of a military force. If administration has found that it can not form an army without conscription, it will find, if it venture on these experiments, that it can not enforce conscription without an army. . . . The Government was not constituted for such purposes. Framed in the spirit of liberty, and the love of peace, it has no powers which render it able to enforce such laws. The attempt, if we rashly make it, will fail; and having already thrown away our peace, we thereby throw away our Government."

—*New Hampshire senator Daniel Webster, speaking against the Conscription Bill of 1814*

others alone, I would also do that." Churches opposed to the war were joined by many abolitionists who saw no purpose to it. The Union had not yet proposed a draft by mid-1862, and many felt it unlikely that the Union ever would, even though the breakaway Confederacy in the South had already done so in April of that year.

Yet that September, the nature of the war—and its relationship to the abolitionist movement—changed dramatically when Lincoln gave the Emancipation Proclamation, granting freedom to all Southern slaves. Almost overnight, the Civil War became about the eradication of slavery. Abolitionists such as William Lloyd Garrison, who just a month earlier had declared his opposition to the war, found themselves supporting it, and pacifist churches, dedicated both to nonviolence and abolition, were now confronted by a crisis of priorities. This crisis came to a head in March 1863, when the Union—faced with growing casualties and a Confederate army that could quickly replace dead or wounded soldiers with new recruits the draft.

The situation was made particularly difficult by the fact that the new draft included no measures exempting conscientious objectors. Although some states (such as Pennsylvania) exempted conscientious objectors from military service provided that they pay a fee "equivalent for personal service," in others they were subject to fines and imprisonment. The first national conscientious objector policy was passed in February 1864, and it allowed objectors to perform noncombatant service by nursing wounded soldiers or assisting recently freed slaves. Most strict pacifists objected to these measures as well. The Quaker magazine *The Friend* hailed the new policy as "a cheering indication of the advance of correct views upon this important subject" but argued that it still unfairly required pacifists to support the war effort. "It matters not," the authors argued, "whether the commutation for military service is money or personal service in some other department; in either case it is an assumption on the part of the government of a right . . . to exact a penalty if he elects to obey God rather than man."

The Confederacy's draft laws were largely similar. Like the Union's draft bill, the Confederate draft regulations of April 1862 included no measures protecting conscientious objectors and left them at the mercy of state law. Some states—particularly Georgia and North Carolina, whose governors were sympathetic to the pacifist

Photograph of a National Guard march from 1899. For the more than 50 years stretching from the end of the Civil War until the beginning of World War I, the United States relied entirely on a volunteer military. *(Library of Congress, Prints and Photographs Division [LC-D4-21210])*

cause—allowed conscientious objectors to perform noncombatant service rather than taking up arms, and as in the Union, some generals chose to exempt conscientious objectors on a case-by-case basis. The Confederacy accommodated many moderate pacifists by formally changing the law in October 1862 to allow individual conscientious objectors to "buy out" of the draft by paying a hefty fine, but those who chose not to do so or could not afford to do so were subject to arrest and generally treated more harshly than their Northern counterparts.

After the Civil War, the draft expired, and the United States switched once again to a professional army, often supported by volunteers from state militias, who had come to be known as the National Guard. This system remained in effect until World War I (1914–18).

A WORLD AT WAR

When the United States entered World War I in 1917, the army once again needed an influx of troops, and the draft was reinstated.

This time, conscientious objectors only had one option—to serve as noncombatants—and by then, most religious pacifists had overcome their objection to indirect support of the war effort. In this respect, the option to serve in a nonmilitary capacity satisfied most objectors.

But those who were pacifists on nonreligious grounds—and religious objectors who did not belong to traditional pacifist churches—faced a tougher hurdle. The 1917 Selective Service regulations protected only conscientious objectors who belonged to "a well-recognized sect or organization organized and existing May 18, 1917, and whose then existing creed or principles forbid its members to participate in war in any form, and whose religious convictions are against war or participation therein in accordance with the creed or principles of said religious organization." Even objectors who arguably met these criteria could still be forced to bear arms or face imprisonment if confronted with unsympathetic draft boards. The more than 5,000 imprisoned World War I draft resisters were sometimes tortured and humiliated, and a few died during their incarceration under suspicious circumstances.

The National Council for Reduction of Armaments held an antiwar rally in 1922. *(Library of Congress, Prints and Photographs Division [LC-USZ62-64294])*

When the war ended, President Woodrow Wilson (1856–1924) granted amnesty to all draft resisters and released them from prison. Although the draft was discontinued until World War II, conscientious objection remained a controversial topic of discussion as the U.S. Supreme Court debated a new issue: pacifist immigrants.

When Rosika Schwimmer immigrated to the United States from Hungary in 1921, she was already known as an influential feminist and pacifist. As former press secretary for the International Woman Suffrage Alliance and cofounder of the Woman's Peace Party, she had played an influential role in the most controversial political debates of her time. When the United States granted women the right to vote in 1920, the nation was regarded as a trailblazer in women's rights and was described as "nearest [to Schwimmer's] ideals of a democratic republic." Schwimmer encountered a problem, however, when she applied for U.S. citizenship: The Oath of Citizenship requires all applicants to agree that they will bear arms on behalf of the United States as necessary. As a conscientious objector, and, perhaps more critically, as a 49-year old woman, Schwimmer would never have been drafted in any previous U.S. war and therefore attempted to exempt herself from the oath's military requirements based on her beliefs. In *United States v. Schwimmer* (1929), the U.S. Supreme Court held that she was bound to agree with the entire oath and rejected her application. Although she continued to reside in the United States for the rest of her life, Schwimmer was never granted U.S. citizenship.

Nor was Douglas Clyde Macintosh, a Baptist minister and Yale University theology professor who had become one of the most well-known religious thinkers of the early 20th century. When Macintosh, a Canadian native, applied for U.S. citizenship, he stated that he would not be willing to swear a general oath declaring his intention to bear arms on behalf of the United States. "I do not undertake to support 'my country, right or wrong' in any dispute which may arise," Macintosh explained, "and I am not willing to promise beforehand, and without knowing the cause for which my country may go to war, either that I will or that I will not 'take up arms in defense of this country.'" The U.S. Supreme Court was not satisfied with this answer, and turned down his application in 1931. It would be another 15 years before

"I am an uncompromising pacifist. . . . If the United States can compel its women citizens to take up arms in the defense of the country—something that no other civilized government has ever attempted—I would not be able to comply with this requirement of American citizenship. In this case I would recognize the right of the Government to deal with me as it is dealing with its male citizens who for conscientious reasons refuse to take up arms."

—*Rosika Schwimmer, as quoted in* United States v. Schwimmer *(1929)*

the Supreme Court addressed the question of pacifist citizenship again, when in *Girouard v. United States* (1946) the U.S. Supreme Court overturned the *Schwimmer* and *Macintosh* precedents by calling on the Immigration and Naturalization Service to waive the duty to bear arms in cases where the prospective citizen objected to all war. A new clause, committing the new citizen to noncombatant service, would later be added to the oath.

World War II began in Europe in 1939, and by 1940, it became clear that the United States could become involved. When the draft was reinstated, it provided the most generous options granted to conscientious objectors in U.S. history. Instead of limiting conscientious objector status to those who held membership in recognized pacifist churches, conscientious objector status was granted to anyone "who, by reason of religious training and belief, is conscientiously opposed to participation in war in any form." Conscientious objectors were asked to serve as noncombatants, and for the first time in U.S. history, pacifists who opposed all participation in war were given a third legal option and "assigned to work of national importance under civilian direction" in Civilian Public Service camps, which were maintained by representatives of pacifist churches. The issue was not entirely resolved, however; civilian registrants were expected to work for free, and more than 15,000 conscientious objectors who opposed all forms of draft registration would be arrested by the end of the war.

In addition to their relative lenience, one other attribute clearly separated the World War II draft regulations from their predecessors: They were the first draft regulations enforced during peacetime. With the exception of one year (1947–48), the U.S. draft was continuously in effect between 1940 and 1973.

> "[Douglas Clyde Macintosh] is unwilling to leave the question of his future military service to the wisdom of Congress where it belongs, and where every native-born or admitted citizen is obliged to leave it. In effect, he offers to take the oath of allegiance only with the qualification that the question whether the war is necessary or morally justified must, so far as his support is concerned, be conclusively determined by reference to his opinion."
>
> —*Supreme Court justice George Sutherland (1862–1942), from his majority ruling in* United States v. Macintosh *(1931)*

Representative Jeannette Rankin (1880–1973) of Montana was one of the most vocal antiwar activists of the 20th century. While serving in Congress (the first woman to do so), she voted against U.S. participation in both World War I and World War II. Years later, in 1968, the 87-year-old Rankin led 5,000 women in a march on the U.S. Capitol to protest the Vietnam War. *(Library of Congress, Prints and Photographs Division [LC-USZ62-66358])*

THE VIETNAM WAR AND THE PEACE MOVEMENT

In addition to being one of the most unpopular U.S. wars of the 20th century, the Vietnam War (1959–75) was also one of the largest in number of troops. In 1965, just over 200,000 U.S. soldiers served in Vietnam; by war's end, that number had increased to more than 2.6 million. In an effort to increase the number of troops that they could dedicate to Vietnam, U.S. military planners boosted the number of draft calls and made it more difficult to obtain a deferment. By war's end, more than 1.7 million U.S. civilians had been drafted into the armed forces.

During the early years of the war, conscientious objector status was still relatively rare, much as it had been during World War II and the Korean War (1950–53). For every 100 civilians drafted, only six were deferred as conscientious objectors. By 1972, 130 conscientious objectors were deferred for every 100 civilians actually called into service. The increase can be traced to two factors: the peace movement and an increasingly liberal definition of conscientious objector status.

The peace movement arose mostly from public dissatisfaction with the Vietnam War and its massive toll of victims. In 1967 alone, more than 11,000 U.S. soldiers had died in Vietnam—more than in the six previous years combined. In 1968, that number increased to more than 16,000. Many were also conscious of the growing number of Vietnamese casualties. A substantial number of Americans—especially young Americans—came to believe that the strategic interests of the United States did not justify such violence, and their frustration with the country's military policy gave birth to a distinctive and powerful antiwar movement. This movement removed the idea of conscientious objection from the margins of American life and placed it squarely in the mainstream.

"As I have walked among the desperate, rejected, and angry young men, I have told them that Molotov cocktails and rifles would not solve their problems. I have tried to offer them my deepest compassion while maintaining that social change comes most meaningfully through non-violent action. But, they asked, what about Vietnam? They asked if our own nation wasn't using massive doses of violence to solve its problems, to bring about the changes it wanted. The question hit home, and I knew that I could never again raise my voice against the violence of the oppressed in the ghettos without having first spoken clearly to the greatest purveyor of violence in the world today, my own government."

—*Martin Luther King, Jr. (1929–68), April 1967*

THE *SEEGER* AND *WELSH* RULINGS

Conscientious objection also received support from the Supreme Court. In two rulings—*United States v. Seeger* (1965) and *Welsh v. United States* (1970)—the Court expanded the definition of conscientious objection to include anyone whose sincere beliefs precluded military service, radically reinterpreting World War II draft regulations that did not protect draftees whose objection to war was based on "political, sociological, or philosophical views or a merely personal moral code."

In the *Seeger* case, the Supreme Court dealt with a draftee who claimed religious conscientious objector status despite being an agnostic. The defendant, Daniel Andrew Seeger, refused to serve in the military because he opposed all war. He was arrested and convicted for refusing the draft but appealed on the grounds that his personal objection to war was tantamount to a religious concern. Although the original draft code specified belief in a "Supreme Being," the Court agreed with Seeger. In a ruling supporting the acquittal, Justice William O. Douglas called attention to the fact that some religions, such as Buddhism, do not affirm the existence of a Supreme Being by any "narrow technical meaning" of the term. He argued that a sophisticated interpretation of conscientious

MUHAMMAD ALI FIGHTS THE DRAFT

In 1966, heavyweight boxing champion and Olympic gold medalist Muhammad Ali was among the more than 300,000 young men drafted into the armed forces. As a Muslim, Ali objected to the Vietnam War as unjust and refused to serve. An outraged public turned on him, the World Boxing Association stripped him of his title, and he was arrested for refusing the draft. Originally sentenced to a five-year prison term, Ali appealed his case all the way to the U.S. Supreme Court. The Court acquitted Ali, ruling that the clumsy and unfair nature of the original conviction invalidated its guilty verdict regardless of whether Ali could technically be classified as a conscientious objector in the traditional sense of the term.

"We have concluded that Congress, in using the expression 'Supreme Being' rather than the designation 'God,' was merely clarifying the meaning of religious training and belief so as to embrace all religions and to exclude essentially political, sociological, or philosophical views. We believe that under this construction, the test of belief 'in relation to a Supreme Being' is whether a given belief that is sincere and meaningful occupies a place in the life of its possessor parallel to that filled by the orthodox belief in God of one who clearly qualifies for the exemption. Where such beliefs have parallel positions in the lives of their respective holders, we cannot say that one is 'in relation to a Supreme Being' and the other is not."

—*Supreme Court justice Tom Clark (1899–1977), from his majority ruling in* United States v. Seeger *(1965)*

objection would acknowledge the "evanescence and fluidity" of the concept of a supreme being as distinct from the philosophical belief in the existence of God. The Court's decision, in other words, was that Seeger's beliefs were religious in character—that they were, in fact, based on some concept of a supreme being—and they therefore qualified him for conscientious objector status.

In the *Welsh* case, the Court went a step further. Elliot Ashton Welsh II claimed conscientious objector status on the explicit grounds that his beliefs, informed by academic theories, should be sufficient to exclude him from the draft. Unlike Seeger, Welsh explicitly stated that his concerns were not religious in nature. This seemed to exclude him from conscientious objector status under both the traditional interpretation of the World War II draft regulations and the broader standard of *Seeger,* which classified some moral beliefs as religious in character. Welsh was convicted for refusing the draft and sentenced to three years in prison. He appealed his case to the Supreme Court, which acquitted him in a controversial ruling. In his majority opinion, Justice Hugo Black (1886–1971) argued that beliefs—whether they are technically religious—should qualify a draftee for conscientious objector status provided that they are held "with the strength of more traditional convictions."

THE FUTURE OF CONSCIENTIOUS OBJECTION

By the time the Vietnam War ended in 1973, U.S. sentiment had turned strongly against the draft. The U.S. military quickly ended the draft and switched to an all-volunteer force. Although young men have been required to register for Selective Service since 1980

WHO IS A CONSCIENTIOUS OBJECTOR?

By 1971, Congress and the Supreme Court had outlined three clear criteria that every conscientious objection claim should meet.

1. The conscientious objection must be to *all* war, not to a specific war. In *Gilette v. United States* (1971), the Supreme Court ruled that no draftee could claim conscientious objector status based on a belief that a specific war was unjust. In his majority ruling, Justice Thurgood Marshall (1908–93) argued that objection to a specific war could not be accommodated by the World War II draft regulations.
2. The conscientious objection must ultimately be religious in character. Under the *Seeger* and *Welsh* rulings, this means that the objection should be based on firm, deeply held beliefs rather than fluid and superficial political judgments.
3. The conscientious objection must be sincere. The conscientious objector must convince the relevant authorities that his concern is an honest and deeply held objection to all war and not merely an attempt to avoid the draft for personal reasons.

and are sometimes prosecuted when they fail to do so, no U.S. citizen has been drafted for more than 30 years.

Today, the idea of the draft remains extremely unpopular. Although one U.S. representative unsuccessfully proposed reinstating the draft in protest against the recent Iraq War (2003), it has been argued that contemporary technology has reduced the need for a large ground army and may have rendered the draft impractical. The long-term fate of the draft remains unknown; the United States has yet to engage in ground combat on the scale seen in Vietnam. Still, unless the draft is reinstated, large-scale conscientious objection to military service will remain a historical issue.

Religion in
Public Schools

The establishment clause of the First Amendment, stating that "Congress shall make no law respecting an establishment of religion," impacts every area of government and public life, but none more so than in the public school system. About 90 percent of American children attend public schools, where they are expected to stay on site for the better part of the five days every week and then take homework with them when they leave. This gives the public school system almost unparalleled control over the lives of children, the most vulnerable and impressionable segment of society. Today, U.S. courts take this factor into account when determining how schools can deal with religion without violating the establishment clause; for example, it is legal for a chaplain to lead Congress in prayer but illegal for a public school teacher to do the same for students. Public school administrators must be extremely cautious not to do anything that imposes religious belief on students.

This is not how the American public school system began, however. Over the past several centuries, the public schools that were originally religious institutions designed to serve a gifted minority have become secular institutions designed to serve all students. The story of how—and why—the U.S. public school system changed is one of the most interesting and controversial in American history.

RELIGION IN THE
U.S. PUBLIC SCHOOL SYSTEM

Until the time of the American Revolution, public schools were primarily intended to promote Christian literacy and prepare students for colleges and universities. These schools were always optional, usually funded at least in part by the parents, generally enrolled a minority of students, and freely mixed religion and the secular curriculum. Although some children attended school, most did not. In this respect most colonial Americans were homeschoolers in that their children were primarily educated at home, and the education of children was considered a parental responsibility. This responsibility was the primary—and for many, the sole—reason that girls were allowed to attend school: Women would be largely responsible for teaching their children.

Reading classes were generally organized around Bible stories, because the most important educational goal for many in the colonies—especially Puritans—was the freedom to read the Bible for themselves. It was this motivation that inspired public school legislation such as the Old Deluder Act, passed by the Massachusetts Bay Colony in 1647, which specifically established religious Bible reading as the primary purpose of public education. Schools also taught students how to write and perform basic mathematics, satisfying the basic requirements of the "three Rs": reading, writing, and arithmetic. Students who wished to go further sometimes had other educational opportunities available to them, but those who wanted to go off to college had to learn Greek and/or Latin first, and their parents generally paid tutors to teach them these languages at home.

During the 18th century, both the number and quality of public schools increased, and students—though still educated primarily at home—were more likely to attend for longer periods of time. By the time of the American Revolution, about 65 percent of men and boys were literate, and an increasing number of girls attended school. And although religion still played a major role in the public school system, the overall purpose of the curriculum was gradually becoming more secular. The Northwest Ordinance of 1787—a document stating basic legal principles for the largely unsettled land that would later become Illinois, Indiana, Michigan, Ohio, and Wisconsin—promoted education not only on the basis of religion itself but also on the grounds of "morality and knowledge."

Still, the average student would attend school for less than three months during an entire lifetime. Shortly after the American Revolution, some political thinkers such as Thomas Jefferson and Benjamin Rush (1745–1813) proposed that education become more

> "It being one chief project of that old deluder, Satan, to keep men from the knowledge of the Scriptures . . . by persuading from the use of tongues, that so that at least the true sense of the original might be clouded and corrupted. . . . It is therefore ordered that every township in this jurisdiction, after the Lord hath increased them to fifty households, shall forthwith appoint one within their town to teach all such children as shall resort to him to write and read."
>
> —*Old Deluder Act (1647), Massachusetts Bay Colony*

"Religion, morality, and knowledge, being necessary to good government and the happiness of mankind, schools and the means of education shall forever be encouraged."

—*Northwest Ordinance (1787)*

universal, largely on the grounds that a democracy cannot function well unless those who vote are guaranteed a reasonably solid education. Because the education of children was seen primarily as a parental responsibility, and because Americans were still celebrating their independence from Britain and were wary of ambitious government programs, the idea of a large, universal, and government-funded public school system did not catch on until the early decades of the 19th century. These new schools, called "common schools," were created in the Northeast primarily to address America's growing immigrant population, which was often poor. Common schools were free, and they were designed to give all students a basic education so that they would be able to hold jobs and fully participate in American life.

Religion still played a major role in common schools, but as the public school system became larger and included a more diverse student body, it also became more secular in many states. Prayer and Bible study, based on Protestant Christian doctrine, were still part of the school day, but the prayers were usually nonspecific and the Bible study usually involved little in-depth reflection. Yet, although religion had become often less pervasive in the curriculum, the early common school religion programs were not inclusive.

There were not many non-Protestants living in the United States during the middle decades of the 19th century, but the Roman Catholic population, for example, was in the process of growing rapidly. Catholic students were essentially excluded from the very Protestant religious activities that took place at common schools, faced a curriculum that was often outspokenly anti-Catholic, and were often subject to ridicule and harassment. To address these problems, Roman Catholic communities began to establish private parochial (church) schools where students could receive a Catholic education. As the Catholic population continued to grow, at the end of the 19th century and the beginning of the 20th century, some legislators were successful in changing common schools to become more tolerant toward Catholics, but the Bible used for study was still the Protestant King James Version (rather than the Douay-Rheims Version used by Catholics), and with some exceptions, the character of religious education at common schools was still Protestant.

"The only foundation for a useful education in a republic is to be laid in religion. Without this, there can be no virtue, and without virtue there can be no liberty, and liberty is the object and life of all republican governments."

—*Benjamin Rush, 1786*

A group of children walk home from a Roman Catholic school in Pittsburgh, Pennsylvania. Parochial schools were an important alternative for Catholic children growing up at a time when most state-funded schools were implicitly Protestant. *(Library of Congress, Prints and Photographs Division [LC-USF33-016124-M4])*

The common school approach had many problems. In addition to excluding Catholics and non-Christians from its religion classes, it did not adequately address the needs of ethnic minorities and was not applied nationwide: For example, the common school approach did not catch on in the South until the early 20th century. Nevertheless, public schools—continually reformed by educational thinkers such as Horace Mann—soon managed to come close to achieving their goals of educating all students who did not attend private schools. In the northeastern United States, about 90 percent of white students attended public schools for at least a few years, and some completed enough schooling to go on to high school, where students studied many of the same subjects that they study in high school today. Women, who were once expected to receive only a minimal education, made up a clear majority of high schools students by 1900 and soon outnumbered men as public school teachers.

THE RIGHT NOT TO ATTEND

The ideal of the universal public school system—in which all Americans participate and in which they are all provided with a common education—was based in part on the theory that it would help bring immigrants into the mainstream of U.S. culture. This principle is eloquently summed up in a 1922 Oregon voter's pamphlet arguing for the Compulsory Education Act, which required all children between the ages of eight and 16 to attend public schools:

> *The assimilation and education of our foreign born citizens . . . are best secured by and through attendance of all children in our public schools. . . . Our children must not under any pretext . . . be divided into antagonistic groups, there to absorb the narrow views of life as they are taught.*

The measure had obvious appeal for at least two groups of people: those who were concerned that immigrants might be forced by circumstances to become second-class citizens and those who wanted to eradicate Roman Catholic parochial schools. With the support of a number of patriotic organizations and the racist Ku Klux Klan, the measure was passed into law and set to take effect in 1926. In response, two very different organizations, the Society of Sisters of the Holy Names of Jesus and Mary and Hill Military Academy, filed suit.

The case was appealed to the U.S. Supreme Court, which struck down the Oregon law in a unanimous 9-0 ruling. Although the First Amendment did not play a role in the verdict (the Supreme Court did not begin applying the First Amendment's religion clauses to state law until 1940), the act was rejected on the grounds that it, in the words of Justice James Clark McReynolds (1862–1946), "unreasonably interferes with the liberty of parents and guardians to direct the upbringing and education of children under their control." He went on to write:

> *The fundamental theory of liberty upon which all governments in this Union repose excludes any general power of the state to standardize its children by forcing them to accept instruction from public teachers only. The child is not the mere creature of the state; those who nurture him and direct his destiny have the right, coupled with high duty, to recognize and prepare him for additional obligations.*

This case, *Pierce v. Society of Sisters* (1925), made it clear that the public school system could not claim a monopoly on education. Legal protection for private schools and homeschooling became even stronger almost 50 years later when, in *Wisconsin v. Yoder* (1972), the Supreme Court cited the First Amendment's free exercise clause in ruling that Amish families (members of a Protestant sect that rejects modern, worldly life) who did not wish to send their children to school past eighth grade could not be forced by law to do so.

By 1920, about one-third of high school–aged Americans attended public high schools. The basic structure of the U.S. public school system had been established, yet it differed in at least one important respect from today's: In most public schools, devotional Bible reading and prayers were still part of the curriculum. Because the Supreme Court had not yet ruled that the Bill of Rights restricts state law, the First Amendment's establishment clause had not been applied to America's public schools.

SCHOOL PRAYER

No single issue related to religion and public schools is more controversial than school prayer, and no issue more clearly reflects the profound changes that have taken place in the area of church and state over the past three centuries. As recently as 50 years ago, prayer in schools, with readings from the Bible, was a common practice dating back to the colonial era. When a series of court rulings removed it from the public school system during the early 1960s, many Americans who had grown up with school prayer were shocked and outraged.

Yet, school prayer had been a controversial issue for quite some time. In 1869, the Board of Education for the Cincinnati public school district, influenced by a bitter struggle between Protestants and Catholics over use of the King James Bible in public schools,

Students at a private school in New Mexico begin their day with a moment of prayer. *(Library of Congress, Prints and Photographs Division [LC-USF34-036592-D])*

passed resolutions banning religious instruction and the devotional reading of religious books, as well as the accompanying hymns. The case was appealed to the Ohio Supreme Court, which ruled in *Board of Education of Cincinnati v. John D. Minor* (1872) that the resolutions were legitimate and could not be struck down by the state court. The court's line of reasoning, as expressed in its majority opinion, is remarkably similar to that of school prayer opponents today:

> *Government is an organization for particular purposes. It is not almighty, and we are not to look to it for everything. The great bulk of human affairs and human interests is left by any free government to individual enterprise and individual action. Religion is eminently one of these interests, lying outside the true and legitimate province of government.*

Conflict between Protestants and Roman Catholics was also the basis for a Chicago school board policy banning in-class Bible reading, which the Illinois Supreme Court upheld in *Ring v. Board of Education* (1910). Still, despite these local rulings, there was no national policy against school prayer and Bible reading, and the vast majority of school districts practiced these customs. Not until 1940 would the U.S. Supreme Court begin applying the First Amendment's religion clauses to state law, and even then, most early cases focused on the free exercise clause.

So it came as a shock to most Americans when the U.S. Supreme Court suddenly banned prayer and devotional Bible reading in all U.S. public school districts with its 6-1 ruling in *Engel v. Vitale* (1962). The case came about as the result of a proposed requirement by the school board of New Hyde Park, New York, that the following nondenominational prayer be recited every morning in front of the teacher:

> *Almighty God, we acknowledge our dependence upon Thee, and we beg Thy blessings upon us, our parents, our teachers and our country.*

Although students were technically permitted to opt out of the prayer, it was nevertheless a government-endorsed prayer and, in the eyes of the Court, a clear violation of the establishment clause. In a similar case, *Abington School District v. Schempp* (1963), the Court ruled that government-sponsored devotional Bible reading is also unconstitutional.

"It is neither sacrilegious nor antireligious to say that each separate government in this country should stay out of the business of writing or sanctioning official prayers and leave that purely religious function to the people themselves and to those the people choose to look to for religious guidance."

—Supreme Court justice Hugo Black, from his majority opinion in Engel v. Vitale *(1962)*

FORCED TO SALUTE

Organized in 1870, the Jehovah's Witnesses are one of the most distinctive and poorly understood Christian denominations in America. Teaching that earthly power is corrupt and subject to evil influence, they conscientiously object to all military service and tend to distrust government authority. This has created friction between the Witnesses and many world governments, especially that of Nazi Germany (which executed thousands of Witnesses in concentration camps as the rest either fled the country or went into hiding) but also that of the United States.

During the early years of World War II, U.S. patriotism was on the rise and laws demanding that schoolchildren salute the flag seemed entirely reasonable to most people. To the Jehovah's Witnesses, though, such laws could not be obeyed. Not only did they suggest submission to an earthly authority, but—especially when accompanied by the Pledge of Allegiance—they seemed obviously idolatrous in that they called on people to hand over their will to an inanimate object.

In 1940, students Lillian Gobitis, aged 12, and her 11-year old brother William, as Jehovah's Witnesses, refused to salute the flag. They were promptly expelled from the school district of Minersville, Pennsylvania.

The Gobitis family appealed all the way to the Supreme Court, which ruled by a surprising 8-1 margin that the children could legally be expelled for refusing to salute the flag.

Partly as a result of the Supreme Court ruling, public sentiment against the Jehovah's Witnesses increased, and some government officials took the verdict as a sign that the group could be legally persecuted. The number of hate crimes against Witnesses increased significantly, and some states began threatening to imprison any children who refused to salute the flag. When the West Virginia Board of Education passed a law patterned after the Minersville law, targeting Jehovah's Witnesses and other children who refused to salute the flag, a Witness named Walter Barnette challenged the new law. His case, too, was appealed to the Supreme Court, which overturned its own recent *Gobitis* verdict by a 6-3 margin, declaring both the new West Virginia law and the old Minersville law to be unconstitutional violations of the First Amendment's free speech clause. The ruling in *West Virginia State Board of Education v. Barnette* (1943) established that children in public schools cannot be forced by law to salute the flag or recite the Pledge of Allegiance, and the ruling has stood ever since.

Since the *Engel* and *Schempp* cases, the Supreme Court has consistently upheld the precedent that government-sponsored school prayer is unconstitutional. The only way that Congress can overrule the Supreme Court is by passing a constitutional amendment, and members of Congress have proposed more than 25 amendments over the past 40 years specifically designed to permit government-sponsored school prayer. All of these proposed amendments have been defeated in Congress.

There has been some indication, however, that the Court does not object to laws establishing a moment of silence during which students may pray. While the Court struck down an Alabama law mandating one minute of silence "for meditation and prayer" in *Wallace v. Jaffree* (1985), several of the majority justices stated that they would be open to the possibility of a moment of silence law not specifically written to accommodate prayer. When Virginia passed just such a law in 2001, a federal court declared it constitutional. The Supreme Court declined to hear the case, leaving the federal court's ruling—and Virginia's moment of silence law—in effect.

CREATIONISM VS. EVOLUTION

Public schools are required to teach science but prohibited from teaching religious doctrine. This seldom produces significant controversy except when a specific religious doctrine is challenged by a scientific theory. Many have argued that no scientific theory has challenged religion in a more direct way than Charles Darwin's theory of evolution.

Until the 20th century, public school science classes did not generally deal with the origins of life in much detail. Origins, when they were discussed, were discussed as a religious topic. Someone attending school before devotional readings were banned in 1963 was probably instructed at least once about the account of creation given in the Bible, which tells the story of God's creation of the world and all life on it in six days.

In his books *On the Origin of Species* (1859) and *The Descent of Man* (1871), British biologist Charles Darwin argued that living things were not created instantly but rather evolved (mutated) slowly, from generation to generation over millions of years. Certain mutations made a creature more likely to survive and produce offspring that would inherit the changes, while other mutations made a creature less likely to survive and produce offspring, which reduced the odds that that mutation would be passed on. Darwin called this theory "natural selection." Most offensive to many people was Darwin's argument that human beings themselves are the product of this process and that human ancestors are monkeys.

In this photograph taken during the landmark 1925 Scopes "monkey trial," defense attorney John R. Neal (center, standing) argues on his client John T. Scopes's behalf as his colleague Clarence Darrow (right) looks on. *(Library of Congress, Prints and Photographs Division [LC-USZ62-105833])*

To most Americans living in the 19th century, Darwin's theory seemed ridiculous. It began to be accepted during the early 20th century, however, and some states began to pass laws banning schoolteachers from telling their students about evolutionary theory. One such law was passed in 1925 by the Tennessee state legislature, which declared that it was illegal for any public school teacher to "teach any theory that denies the story of the divine creation of man as taught in the Bible, and to teach instead that man has descended from a lower order of animals." A young biology teacher named John T. Scopes was arrested under this law, and the resulting trial—called the Scopes trial, or "monkey trial"—captured the attention of the entire country during the summer of 1925. Scopes was found guilty under the law and fined $100 by the judge, but he appealed the case to a higher court, and it was overturned on a technicality. The Tennessee antievolution law, which had been ridiculed by the national press and quickly became an embarrassment to the state, was never enforced again. In *Epperson v. Arkansas* (1968), the U.S. Supreme Court declared all antievolution laws to be unconstitutional under the First Amendment's establishment clause.

In the years since the Scopes trial, evolutionary theory has become almost universally accepted among biologists. After the Supreme Court banned devotional Bible reading and other forms of religious instruction, it became impossible to teach the biblical account of creation as a religious doctrine. Faced with this limitation, opponents of evolutionary theory described the biblical account as a scientific position called "creationism" and attempted to add it to public school science courses. The Balanced Treatment Act, passed by the Louisiana state legislature in 1985, required school science teachers to grant "equal time" to creationism and evolutionary theory. The law was challenged and appealed to the Supreme Court in *Edwards v. Aguillard* (1987), and the Court ruled that laws requiring the teaching of creationism violate the establishment clause by promoting a religious doctrine as science.

Although the controversy over evolutionary theory has largely died down, there have been some recent events that suggest that the issue is far from resolved. In 1999, the Kansas Board of Education removed evolutionary theory from the state science curriculum requirements. After public outcry and a series of new school board elections, the Kansas board returned evolutionary theory to the science curriculum in 2001.

Over the past decade, a number of state legislatures have also proposed—and, in a few cases, passed—laws that require public school science textbooks to include disclaimers stating the limitations of evolutionary theory and sometimes to include brief critiques as part of the disclaimer. There is also a growing movement among religious conservatives to promote intelligent design theory, which bears a strong resemblance to creationism but makes no specific religious claims, and conservatives therefore hope it might one day be taught in public school science classes.

PRIVATE SCHOOLS AND PUBLIC MONEY

Although the debates over school prayer and creationism versus evolution still rage, the Supreme Court has rendered clear verdicts in both issues that are based on sound precedents and will be difficult to overturn. Such is not the case with another contemporary controversy, the issue of private school vouchers (sometimes called "school choice"), by which students may opt out of public school and attend private school, with the money that would have been used to finance their public school education applied toward their tuition. Because most private schools are operated by religious organizations and are not bound by the establishment clause, vouchers lead to a scenario in which the federal government is paying tuition for religious instruction.

Early rulings dealing with public assistance to private schools depended primarily on the answer to one question: Does the proposed assistance help individual students without providing any direct benefits to religious institutions? If the answer was yes, the Supreme Court generally approved the policy. This was the case with *Everson v. Board of Education* (1947), in which the Court held that New Jersey could provide public transportation for children attending private schools, and *Board of Education v. Allen* (1968), in which the Court approved a New York program that loaned books to private school students. If the answer was no, however, the Supreme Court generally rejected the policy. This was the case in *Lemon v. Kurtzman* (1971). The Court's ruling applied to three cases challenging two laws, a Pennsylvania law that permitted the state to pay the salaries of some private school teachers and purchase textbooks and other teaching supplies on their behalf, and a Rhode Island law that required the state to pay 15 percent of each private school teacher's salary. In an 8-0 ruling, the Court held that all of the policies were unconstitutional. In the process, the Court established a standard called the *Lemon* test, which holds that a law does not violate the establishment clause if it has a legitimate secular (nonreligious) purpose, if it does not have the primary effect of advancing or inhibiting religion, and if it does not excessively entangle religion and government.

The standards set forth in *Lemon v. Kurtzman* are still accepted today by most members of the Supreme Court and have been particularly relevant to the school vouchers issue, which the Court has addressed twice in recent years. *Mueller v. Allen* (1983) dealt with a Minnesota law that gave tax credit for education expenses, even those pertaining to private school tuition—not precisely a voucher proposal, but remarkably similar to one in that it indirectly paid for religious instruction. Writing for a 5-4 majority, Justice William Rehnquist argued that the Minnesota law did not violate the *Lemon*

"The [Cleveland vouchers] program does not force any individual to submit to religious indoctrination or education. It simply gives parents a greater choice as to where and in what manner to educate their children. This is a choice that those with greater means have routinely exercised."

—*Supreme Court justice Clarence Thomas, from his concurring opinion in* Zelman v. Simmons-Harris *(2002)*

test: It had a legitimate secular purpose, it did not advance religion ("the deduction is available for educational expenses incurred by all parties"), and did not excessively entangle religion and government. The *Mueller* ruling contradicted the Court's decision in *Committee for Public Education and Religious Liberty v. Nyquist* (1972), in which it held that a similar New York law violated the establishment clause.

Yet the idea of school vouchers—direct assistance to parents, to be used to pay for private school tuition—was not tested in the Supreme Court until *Zelman v. Simmons-Harris* (2002). The case dealt with an Ohio law that allowed students in Cleveland, where the public school system did not adequately serve the needs of many students, to receive financial assistance from the state that could be used to attend private schools. In a razor-thin 5-4 ruling, written once again by Chief Justice William Rehnquist, the Court held that the Ohio law does not violate the *Lemon* test because it has a legitimate secular purpose (in that it serves the basic educational needs of students in Cleveland), does not advance religion ("the Ohio program is neutral in all respects towards religion"), and does not excessively entangle religion and government ("the incidental advancement of a religious mission . . . is reasonably attributable to the individual aid recipients [and] not the government"). The Court held that, although 96 percent of students who used Ohio's vouchers attended religious schools, decisions regarding which schools to attend were nevertheless left to the individual students and their parents. The amount of the tuition voucher would be the same whether the private school was operated by a religious organization or not.

Encouraged by the *Zelman* ruling, other states, such as Florida, have announced new school voucher proposals. Yet vouchers are very much a political issue. Supporters believe that vouchers will help gifted low-income students escape from underfunded public schools and force failing public schools to improve so that they can compete with private schools for students. Opponents argue that vouchers are a violation of the establishment clause and weaken the public school system by spending educational funds on private school tuition. It is likely that the debate over school vouchers will not be settled for years to come.

7

Freedom from Religion?

The First Amendment to the Constitution begins with 10 words that are known as the establishment clause: "Congress shall make no law respecting an establishment of religion . . ." Most disagreements over the role religion should play in government can be reduced to debates over what this establishment clause means. Does it refer only to a state church, such as the Church of England, or does it refer to a state religion? If it does refer to a state religion, does this mean that the government cannot endorse religious beliefs, such as belief in the existence of God?

Because of the sweeping Supreme Court rulings that have come down over the past 40 years in favor of full separation of church and state, many believe that the controversy over the role or religion in U.S. government is a new one, brought about by the social reforms of the 1960s. In fact, the debate is older than the U.S. government itself.

A RELIGIOUS AND SECULAR NATION

Nearly all of the first American colonists favored some form of religious government, and the charters of all 13 original colonies cite Christianity as an official, or at least implicit, religion. Christianity was reflected in the laws of the colonies, most of which had no separation of church and state.

During the 18th century, an increasing number of American political philosophers were influenced by the philosophy of the Enlightenment, a movement originating in Europe that favored secular governments. The Enlightenment was generally hostile

> "I contemplate . . . that act of the whole American people which declared that their legislature should 'make no law respecting an establishment of religion, or prohibiting the free exercise thereof,' thus building a wall of separation between Church and State."
>
> —*Thomas Jefferson, letter to Danbury Baptist Association (January 1, 1802)*

In 1797, John Adams signed the Treaty of Tripoli, which was unanimously passed by the U.S. Senate. The treaty states in part that "the government of the United States is not in any sense founded on the Christian Religion." *(Library of Congress, Prints and Photographs Division [LC-USZ62-13002])*

toward the official government churches that dominated Europe at the time and sometimes hostile toward religion itself, though most philosophers of the Enlightenment did believe in God. The authors of the Constitution and the Bill of Rights were generally much more liberal on religious issues than were most Americans, most of whom had not studied Enlightenment philosophers, and nearly all of the founding fathers worshipped God and attended church regularly, regardless of their specific religious beliefs. Thomas Jefferson's Declaration of Independence states that it is the "Creator" rather than a government that grants human rights, yet the document makes no reference to Christianity. The Constitution itself does not mention God.

Legal scholars debate what the founding fathers meant to say when they passed the establishment clause. For his part, Jefferson, the man responsible for convincing James Madison to propose the First Amendment in the first place, believed that the establishment clause built "a wall of separation between Church and State." And in the 1797 Treaty of Tripoli, passed by the U.S. Senate and signed by President John Adams, the United States assures the Muslim government of Libya that the U.S. government "is not in any sense founded on the Christian religion" and has no objection to Islam.

Still, the vast majority of Americans living during the 18th and 19th centuries were Christians. This was formally recognized by the Supreme Court in *Holy Trinity Church v. United States* (1892), in which the Court reviewed an anti-immigrant law prohibiting organizations from actively encouraging citizens from other countries to work for them in the United States. When a U.S. church attempted to hire a priest living in England, it was

"As the Government of the United States of America is not in any sense founded on the Christian religion; as it has in itself no character of enmity against the laws, religion, or tranquillity, of [Muslims]; and as the said States never have entered into any war or act of hostility against any [Muslim] nation, it is declared by the parties that no pretext arising from religious opinions shall ever produce an interruption of the harmony existing between the two countries."

—*Treaty of Tripoli, 1797*

prosecuted under the law—and promptly challenged that law all the way to the Supreme Court. In his majority ruling, Justice David Brewer (1837–1910) struck down the portion of the law applying to ministers and other skilled laborers, believing it to be particularly irrelevant when applied to ministers because "[America] is a Christian nation." In his book *The United States: A Christian Nation* (1905), Justice Brewer explained that he was referring to America's character, not its government:

> We classify nations . . . by Religion. One is a [Muslim] nation, others are heathen, and still others are Christian nations. . . . But in what sense can [America] be called a Christian nation? Not in the sense that Christianity is the established religion or that people are in any matter compelled to support it. . . . In fact, the government as a legal organization is independent of all religions.

Still, the U.S. government of the 19th century was in many ways less secular than it is today. Bible classes were taught in public schools; schools also held official morning prayers. Laws specifically written with Christians in mind—such as laws requiring all businesses to close on Sundays—were common. Government monuments constructed at the time frequently referred to God and occasionally to biblical figures (though specific references to Jesus Christ were fairly rare). This continued well into the 1950s, when lawmakers affirmed the existence of God on coins and in the Pledge of Allegiance to distinguish the United States from its cold war foe, the antireligious Soviet Union.

THREE SCHOOLS OF THOUGHT

A series of Supreme Court rulings secularized many aspects of the U.S. government over the past 50 years, provoking some to protest and others to call for more secularization. There are essentially three points of view on the relationship between religion and the government, as expressed in the establishment clause: preferentialism, separationism, and accommodationism.

- ◆ **Preferentialists** believe that the government is well within its rights to write laws that affirm—or prefer—Christianity, provided that it does not establish its own churches. Although some lawmakers in the conservative wing of the Republican

THE *LEMON* TEST

In *Lemon v. Kurtzman* (1971), the Supreme Court struck down several laws that paid the salaries of some teachers at private schools. As part of the ruling, Chief Justice Warren Burger (1907–95), a separationist, established a three-part standard—the *Lemon* test—that has been used by the Court for more than 30 years to determine whether a law violates the establishment clause.

1. Does the law have a legitimate secular purpose? According to the *Lemon* test, the answer to this question is yes. If a law is written to serve a purely religious purpose, it is a violation of the establishment clause.
2. Does the law have the primary effect of advancing or inhibiting religion? According to the *Lemon* test, the answer to this question is no. Any law that has the primary effect of either advancing or inhibiting religion is a violation of the establishment clause.
3. Does the law excessively entangle religion and government? According to the *Lemon* test, the answer to this question is also no. Even if a law has a secular purpose and does not have the primary effect of advancing or inhibiting religion, its usefulness should be weighed against the risk it creates by involving the government in religious matters.

Party are preferentialists, most judges are not; the Supreme Court has never affirmed preferentialism in a ruling, and none of its current justices supports it.

♦ **Separationists** believe in Jefferson's "wall of separation between Church and State." They hold that the government cannot endorse Christianity or any other religion and that Congress should write neutral laws that do not support religion in any direct way. Many lawmakers are strict separationists (especially within the Democratic Party), and it has been the dominant position of the Supreme Court over the past 50 years.

◆ **Accommodationists** believe that the First Amendment prevents the government from writing laws that affirm or prefer Christianity but does not prevent laws that assist religious organizations as long as all religions are treated equally. Several members of the Supreme Court are accommodationists, as are many lawmakers (especially within the Republican Party).

The two central controversies over government secularization deal with the funding of religious charities and references to God in official government contexts.

THE FAITH-BASED INITIATIVE

One controversial question being asked today is, To what extent can the government fund religious organizations that serve secular needs? Traditionally, federal funding has been available primarily for secular charities. Religious charities could be eligible for federal fund-

The Salvation Army is both a religious denomination and one of the most widely respected charities in the United States. Here, a group of Salvation Army volunteers brings refreshments to soldiers returning from World War I. *(National Archives and Records Administration [ARC 533625])*

> "Public funding of faith-based institutions is one of those rare proposals that harms virtually everyone affected by it. The initiative promotes publicly funded employment discrimination, it threatens the religious liberty of beneficiaries, it jeopardizes the freedom of our faith communities and it undermines the rights of all taxpayers."
>
> —*Reverend Barry W. Lynn, president of Americans United for Separation of Church and State, 2002*

ing, but only if they were operated separately as if they were secular charities and were willing to hire employees of any faith. Charities operated by the Salvation Army, for example, have received federal funding for their work on behalf of the poor, but the Salvation Army itself would not have been eligible for federal funding.

This changed on August 22, 1996, when President Bill Clinton signed the Personal Responsibility and Work Opportunity Reconciliation Act into law. Although the act deals primarily with the welfare system, it also includes a section called Charitable Choice, which allows religious charities to receive government funding under the following conditions:

- The funds may not be used for religious purposes.
- Charities may not practice religious discrimination in the way they conduct their work (though they may discriminate on the basis of religion when hiring staff).
- Secular alternatives must always be available so that members of the community who object to being served by a religious charity may have their needs met elsewhere.

In January 2001, President George W. Bush established the White House Office of Faith-Based and Community Initiatives to encourage greater cooperation between the government and private charities. President Bush has also supported legislation that would go further in encouraging faith-based charities to apply for government funding, an effort that is referred to as the faith-based initiative. The effort has met with some criticism from separationists, who are concerned that government funding of religious organizations is exactly what the First Amendment was intended to prevent.

THE PLEDGE OF ALLEGIANCE

In 1892, a Baptist minister named Francis Bellamy (1855–1932) wrote the Pledge of Allegiance to be recited by schoolchildren on the 400th anniversary of Columbus's arrival in America. Public schools across the country quickly began using the pledge as a daily practice, and it was soon adopted by the U.S. public school system as an official declaration of patriotism.

The wording of the pledge was changed several times during the early 20th century. Most striking was the addition of the phrase *under*

In this 1942 photograph, children at a school in Southington, Connecticut, pledge allegiance to the U.S. flag "and to the republic for which it stands: one nation, indivisible, with liberty and justice for all." The phrase "under God" was not added to the Pledge of Allegiance until 1954. *(Library of Congress, Prints and Photographs Division [LC-USW3-042032-E])*

> "I pledge allegiance to my Flag and to the Republic for which it stands: one Nation indivisible, with Liberty and Justice for all."
>
> —*Francis Bellamy, Pledge of Allegiance (1892)*

God in 1954, which Congress added in order to "further acknowledge the dependence of our people and our Government upon the moral directions of the Creator" and "deny the atheistic and materialistic concepts of communism." In 1955, Congress passed a law requiring that the phrase *In God We Trust* appear on all U.S. currency, and in 1956, "In God We Trust" became the U.S. national motto.

Almost 50 years later, in June 2002, the U.S. Court of Appeals for the Ninth Circuit—a large court representing nine states, including California—ruled that the phrase *under God* violates the establishment clause. The case was brought about by Michael New-

> "I pledge allegiance to the flag of the United States of America and to the Republic for which it stands, one Nation under God, indivisible, with liberty and justice for all."
>
> —*Pledge of Allegiance, as it is recited today*

STATE-SPONSORED HOLIDAY DECORATIONS

No single holiday is more widely celebrated in American culture than Christmas. Although it has its origins in the Christian celebration of the birth of Jesus Christ, it has also become an important secular holiday—a time of the year when friends and family members, many of whom do not belong to the Christian faith, exchange gifts with one another. It is also a time of publicly affirming sentiments of goodwill, generosity, and peace. The Jewish holiday of Hanukkah, an eight-day festival celebrating an ancient revolt against an oppressive government; the Islamic holiday of Eid al-Fitr, the feast that concludes the month-long fast called Ramadan; Kwanzaa, a seven-day harvest festival based on African traditions; and the New Year also occur at roughly the same time of year as Christmas, fostering an overall celebratory spirit.

If a local government wishes to display holiday decorations in a courthouse or another government building—setting up a Christmas tree, for example, or depictions of Santa Claus or elves—then this is usually less controversial, due to Christmas's status as an important secular holiday. Celebrating the religious bases of Christmas and other holidays, on the other hand, can create some establishment clause issues. When is it acceptable for a government to display a nativity scene depicting the birth of Jesus or a menorah celebrating the eight days of Hanukkah?

The Supreme Court addressed this issue in *Allegheny v. ACLU* (1989), which dealt with two holiday displays in Pittsburgh, Pennsyl-vania: a nativity scene set up alone on the grand staircase of the county courthouse, and a Hanukkah menorah set up outside a government building alongside a Christmas tree and a sign saluting liberty. The Court held that the nativity scene was unconstitutional, but the menorah was not. Under an interpretation that some half-jokingly call the "plastic reindeer doctrine," religious holiday decorations on official government property are acceptable if they are presented alongside secular holiday decorations. In his majority ruling, Justice Harry Blackmun (1908–99) held that religious decorations, when presented alongside other decorations in a way that does not suggest government endorsement of a specific faith, are "understood as conveying the city's secular recognition of different traditions for celebrating the winter-holiday season."

A nativity scene, the Christmas Cave of Bethlehem, at Mercy Hospital in Baltimore, Maryland *(Library of Congress, Prints and Photographs Division [LC-USZ62-98161])*

dow, an atheist (a person who does not believe in God) arguing on behalf of his daughter, who was expected to recite the pledge with her classmates. When the case was appealed by the School district to the Supreme Court in *Elk Grove Unified School District v. Newdow* (2004), the Court overruled the circuit court's decision on a technicality: The justices argued that Newdow did not have legal standing to sue on behalf of his daughter due to the custody arrangement between him and his ex-wife. The Court as a whole, therefore, did not address the question of whether the use of *under God* in the pledge actually violates the establishment clause. It is extremely probable that at some point soon, another parent—one who has full custody over his or her child—will challenge the Pledge of Allegiance, and the Supreme Court will consider this issue.

This case would be important not only because of how it might change the Pledge of Allegiance but also because of its potential impact on other official uses of the word *God*. If the Court rules that the use of *under God* is unconstitutional in the Pledge of Allegiance, many other national symbols may be changed, including the phrase *In God We Trust*. The motto was itself inspired by the national anthem, *The Star-Spangled Banner*, which includes the lines:

> *Blest with victory and peace, may the heaven-rescued land*
> *Praise the Power that hath made and preserved us a nation.*
> *Then conquer we must, when our cause it is just,*
> *And this be our motto: "In God is our trust."*

On the other hand, if the Supreme Court affirms that references to God do not violate the establishment clause, then it is likely that many lawmakers will support newer, lengthier, and more direct government-endorsed references to God. This would further exclude a group of Americans who often go ignored in discussions of religious liberty.

THE FREEDOM FROM RELIGION MOVEMENT

According to the City University of New York's 2001 American Religious Identification Survey, about 29.5 million Americans—more than 14 percent of the population—do not belong to any religion. This number has steadily increased over the past 35

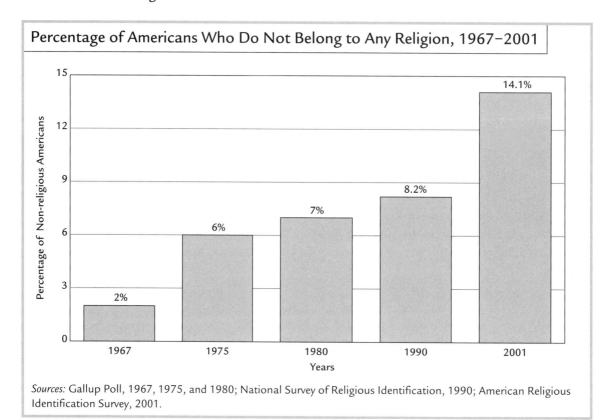

Percentage of Americans Who Do Not Belong to Any Religion, 1967–2001

Sources: Gallup Poll, 1967, 1975, and 1980; National Survey of Religious Identification, 1990; American Religious Identification Survey, 2001.

years; in 1967, only 2 percent of Americans claimed not to belong to any religion.

There have always been nonreligious Americans, but they have routinely faced legal discrimination. For the first centuries of American history, Christianity was endorsed by many sectors of the U.S. government. Public schools, for example, included Bible classes and prayers. Conscientious objector status—granted to those who were drafted to serve in the military but whose beliefs prohibited it—was granted only to members of organized faiths. For the 5 to 10 percent of Americans who in addition to not belonging to any religion do not believe in God, patriotic symbols that other Americans take for granted—such as the phrase *In God We Trust,* which appears on every piece of currency—can seem like official statements that these nonbelievers are second-class citizens and not full participants in American life. Those who do not believe in God also face significant public prejudice; according to a 2002 survey conducted by the Pew Forum on Religion and Public Life, 54 percent of

Americans have an unfavorable opinion of atheists. For his part, Thomas Jefferson, in his *Notes on the State of Virginia* (1780), specifically included atheists among those whose freedom he would protect ("It does me no injury," he wrote, "for my neighbor to say there are twenty gods or no god").

Over the past 40 years, great strides have been made in what has been called the freedom from religion movement, the movement to prevent government endorsement of religion over nonreligion. In a series of highly controversial rulings during the early 1960s, the Supreme Court struck down government-sanctioned prayer and Bible reading in public school and, during the Vietnam War, reinterpreted draft regulations to include conscientious objectors who do not hold traditional religious beliefs.

Although the freedom from religion movement has made significant progress, it still faces serious challenges posed by the faith-based initiative, private school vouchers, and references to God made in an official government context. The public and political opposition that nonreligious Americans regularly face would make reform on these issues impossible were it not for the broader separationist movement that also discourages government endorsement of religion. Much of the success of the freedom from religion movement will depend on two factors: whether nonreligious Americans gain power as a political force and whether the Supreme Court remains primarily separationist.

A World War II poster: "This is America . . . where you pray to God in your own way, according to your own beliefs, in the peace and blessing of religious tolerance." Atheists and agnostics were welcomed under Thomas Jefferson's ideal of religious liberty but have often been excluded from mainstream American culture. *(National Archives and Records Administration [ARC 515774])*

Religious Liberty around the World

Even before the United States had a bill of rights, it was clear that it would take a radically new approach to the relationship between religion and government. The word God appeared nowhere in the U.S. Constitution, and there were no references to an official religion of any kind. Religious oaths and doctrine tests, required in many governments for those who wished to hold public office, were clearly forbidden. This was in sharp contrast to the other nations of the time, all of which had some sort of government-supported religion. Many historians have argued that the United States was the first secular national government on Earth, and it certainly produced the first modern, completely secular system of law and government.

Today, the U.S. model is no longer unique. The U.S. policy on the relationship between religion and government is now regarded as moderate, more religious than some but less religious than others. This chapter will discuss four different kinds of religion-government relationships:

- Secular governments that regulate religion, represented in this chapter by North Korea. Governments that fall into this category generally follow communist principles similar to those of China and the former Soviet Union. They have no official religion but restrict the activity of religious organizations not sponsored by the government.
- Secular governments with religious liberty, represented in this chapter by France. Other examples include the United States and Japan.
- Religious governments with religious liberty, represented in this chapter by Bolivia. These governments have an official religion

THE ROLE OF THE UNITED NATIONS

In response to religious persecution pursued by both secular and religious governments, the United Nations passed the Declaration on the Elimination of All Forms of Intolerance and of Discrimination Based on Religion or Belief in 1981. Although the declaration is nonbinding, it establishes a clear set of rights that the United Nations has officially agreed to promote:

- The right to hold both public and private worship
- The right to establish religious charities and fund-raising organizations
- The right to make, own, and use ceremonial religious items
- The right to publish and distribute religious material
- The right to teach religious classes
- The right to ask for donations
- The right to select one's own religious leaders
- The right to celebrate religious holidays
- The right to communicate with others about religion and religious concerns, both nationally and internationally

The number of countries that practice severe religious oppression seems to be slowly declining. The collapse of the Soviet Union in 1991 essentially prevented the further growth of communism, which until that time was widely regarded as the most serious political threat to religious liberty.

but allow other religions to coexist. Another example is the United Kingdom.
- Religious governments with religious regulation, represented in this chapter by Saudi Arabia. These governments have an official religion and restrict the activities of other religious groups.

NORTH KOREA
SECULAR GOVERNMENT WITH RELIGIOUS REGULATION

The end of World War II, in 1945, brought about the liberation of Korea from decades of Japanese rule. After the war, the victorious

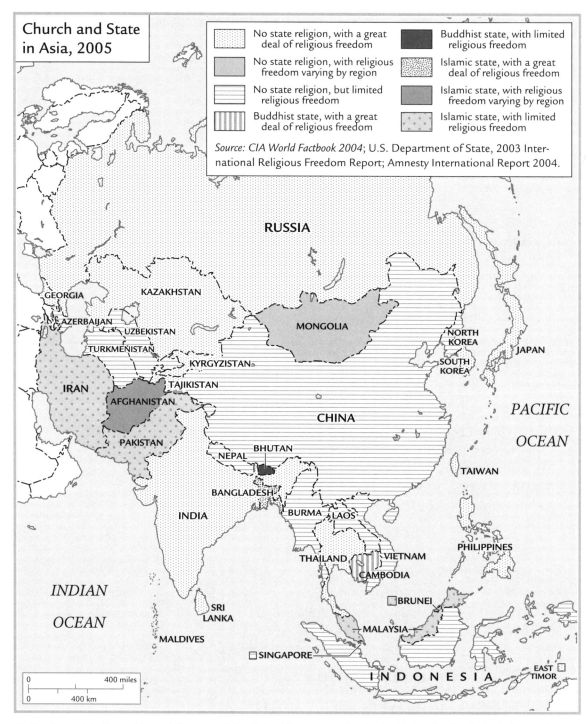

Church and State in Asia, 2005

Legend:

- No state religion, with a great deal of religious freedom
- No state religion, with religious freedom varying by region
- No state religion, but limited religious freedom
- Buddhist state, with a great deal of religious freedom
- Buddhist state, with limited religious freedom
- Islamic state, with a great deal of religious freedom
- Islamic state, with religious freedom varying by region
- Islamic state, with limited religious freedom

Source: CIA World Factbook 2004; U.S. Department of State, 2003 International Religious Freedom Report; Amnesty International Report 2004.

Owing in part to the cold war influence of the United States and the Soviet Union, both of which favored secular governments, most governments in Asia have no official state religion, while some tend to favor Buddhism or Islam. Religious freedom became more widespread in Asia following the reform and subsequent collapse of the Soviet Union (which opposed all religion), but some countries—such as North Korea and China—on this extremely diverse continent still practice religious oppression.

U.S. and Soviet forces divided Korea in half: The United States would establish a government south of the 38th parallel, while the Soviet-Union would establish a government to the north. The U.S.-backed government of South Korea was a republic; the Soviet-backed government of North Korea was a Communist State. After the Korean War (1950–53), in which North Korea launched a surprise attack on South Korea, the two nations were divided along a demarcation (separation) line: North Korea (officially the Democratic People's Republic of Korea) has remained Communist, while South Korea (the Republic of Korea) established a democratic system of government patterned after that of the United States. Although there has been some talk in recent years of reunifying Korea, the prospects seem remote.

North Korea has one of the most oppressive governments on Earth. Spoken criticism of the government or gathering information through unofficial channels (such as nongovernment news sources) can be classified as "suppressing the national liberation struggle . . . in collusion with imperialists," "ideological divergence," and "opposing socialism"—crimes that carry the death penalty. Torture is also frequently used. According to a report from the U.S. State Department, North Korean prisons once had, and may still have, policies forbidding live births. Infants born to women in prison have been executed, and this practice is sometimes carried out in front of the mother as a form of torture. North Korean citizens are forbidden by law to access the Internet or make international telephone calls except under special circumstances and with government approval. In addition to policies restricting the behavior of its own citizens, the North Korean government has kidnapped hundreds of citizens from South Korea and Japan.

North Korea's official position on religion as stated in its constitution is that it permits "freedom of religious belief" and "the right to build buildings for religious use." In practice, only a few formal churches exist, and they are heavily monitored and regulated by the government; international visitors report that sermons always seem to focus on praise and support of the North Korean government. Although reliable statistics on North Korean religious identity are not available, the U.S. Central Intelligence Agency has estimated that about 26 percent of North Koreans identify as Christian, 26 percent as Buddhist, and 46 percent claim no religious affiliation. Most religious communities in North Korea are underground "house churches," which the North Korean

"No one may use religion as a means by which to drag in foreign powers or to destroy the state or social order."

—*From the Constitution of North Korea*

RELIGIOUS LIBERTY IN JAPAN

In 1947, the United States and its allies drafted a new constitution for Japan to replace the imperial government that had collapsed in the aftermath of World War II. The imperial government was in many respects a merged church-state institution, as it formally recognized the traditional Japanese religion of Shinto and declared the emperor to be a living god. To prevent a new religious government from forming, Articles 20 and 89 of the new Japanese constitution were written to guarantee freedom of religion and separation of church and state in extremely clear terms:

> No religious organization shall receive any privileges from the state or exercise any political authority. No person shall be compelled to take part in any religious acts. The state and its organs shall refrain from religious education or any other religious activity. . . . No public money or other property shall be appropriated for the use, benefit, or maintenance of any religious institution or association for any charitable, educational, or benevolent enterprises not under the control of public authority.

The status of religious liberty in Japan is essentially identical to its status in the United States. Japanese political leaders are, however, held to a different standard: While U.S. political leaders campaign partly on the basis of their religious beliefs and frequently cite those beliefs in speeches, Japanese politi-cians are expected to avoid engaging in any religious behavior while acting as agents of the government. In 2004, a Japanese district court ruled that Prime Minister Junichiro Koizumi's visit to a Shinto shrine—in which he used a government car and signed the guest book with his official government signature—violated Article 20 ("the state and its organs shall refrain from . . . [any] religious activity") of the Japanese constitution, but it did not punish him. Although Japanese politicians are given the same religious freedoms as other citizens in their private lives, they are expected not to use any government resources when participating in religious activities.

A Shinto priestess prepares a ritual offering. *(Library of Congress, Prints and Photographs Division [LC-USZ62-95824])*

government usually tolerates as long as its members make no organized attempt to evangelize. Those who do are subject to imprisonment, torture, and possible execution.

FRANCE
Secular Government with Religious Liberty

As the United States voted on the Bill of Rights in 1789, the French Revolution (1789–99) began. Public opposition had built up against the government, headed by kings who believed themselves to be chosen by God and corrupt leaders of the national Catholic Church who sometimes wielded enormous political power in their own right. The French people overthrew their king and established a republic based on the Declaration of the Rights of Man, a document that was patterned after the U.S. Declaration of Independence and also bears many similarities to the U.S. Bill of Rights. The experience of French revolutionaries, who

This sketch depicts priests who refused to pledge allegiance to the government in the years immediately following the French Revolution. *(Library of Congress, Prints and Photographs Division [LC-USZ62-97553])*

> "No one shall be disquieted on account of his opinions, including his religious views, provided their manifestation does not disturb the public order established by law."
>
> —*From the* Declaration of the Rights of Man *(1789)*

had suffered at the hands of a corrupt church-state government, led to the concept of *laïcité* (secularism), the idea that the political power of religious institutions should be kept in check by the government. The new French government reacted strongly—and sometimes violently—against the existing church establishment, culminating in the bloody Reign of Terror (1793–94), in which many former political and religious leaders were executed. Although France's government has changed many times since the revolution, it has consistently returned to the concept of a secular republic with an extremely solid separation of church and state.

Today, those guiding principles inform the French republic. Religious freedom in France is similar in many respects to religious freedom in the United States, with some exceptions. The French government closely monitors 173 "minority cults," including the Jehovah's Witnesses and the Church of Scientology, watching out for behavior ranging from "fraud and falsifications" to "psycholgical or physical subjection."

The French government also deals with religious expression in a slightly different way. While U.S. First Amendment is primarily concerned with preventing a government establishment of religion, French law is concerned about any consolidation of religious power that could have a dangerous effect on public order. For this reason, the French legislature passed a law in 2004 against all religious symbols worn to school. Many believed that its intent was to ban Muslim girls from wearing headscarves in public schools. Many supporters of the law were concerned that headscarves segregate Muslims from the broader French community and encourage

THE UNITED KINGDOM
An Unfunded Establishment

Although the Church of England and the Church of Scotland are still the official churches of the United Kingdom, they are self-supporting and receive no special government funding. Their role, like the monarchy, has become largely ceremonial. They do, however, play a central role in English and Scottish culture and in the cultures of other churches throughout the world. The Church of England, in particular, is the central authority of the Anglican Communion, a network of 77 million Anglicans (Episcopalians) worldwide.

Church and State in Europe, 2005

Legend	
No state religion, with a great deal of religious freedom	Lutheran state, with a great deal of religious freedom
No state religion, with religious freedom varying by region	Joint Lutheran and Eastern Orthodox state, with a great deal of religious freedom
No state religion, but limited religious freedom	Eastern Orthodox state, with a great deal of religious freedom
Anglican state, with a great deal of religious freedom	Eastern Orthodox state, with limited religious freedom

Source: CIA World Factbook 2004; U.S. Department of State, 2003, International Religious Freedom Report; Amnesty International Report 2004.

ICELAND

ATLANTIC

OCEAN

NORWEGIAN SEA

NORWAY

SWEDEN

FINLAND

ESTONIA

RUSSIA

SCOTLAND

NORTH SEA

DENMARK

LATVIA

LITHUANIA

RUSSIA

IRELAND

BARENTS SEA

BELARUS

WALES ENGLAND

NETHERLANDS

POLAND

UKRAINE

BELGIUM GERMANY

LUXEMBOURG

CZECH REP.

SLOVAKIA

MOLDOVA

FRANCE

Bay of Biscay

SWITZERLAND AUSTRIA HUNGARY

SLOVENIA CROATIA ROMANIA

BLACK SEA

PORTUGAL

ANDORRA

BOSNIA HERZEGOVINA SERBIA AND MONTENEGRO BULGARIA

SPAIN

ITALY

MACEDONIA

ALBANIA

TURKEY

MEDITERRANEAN SEA

GREECE

MALTA

0   500 miles

0   500 km

Most countries on this map of Europe have secular governments with no state religion, but several denominations of Christianity—the Anglican and Eastern Orthodox Churches, as well as several Protestant denominations—still receive government endorsement. Religious freedom is relatively common in Europe, though a few countries—such as Bulgaria, the former Baltic Republic of Belarus, and regions of Bosnia-Herzegovina—still restrict religious practice.

hostility toward French customs in France's large Muslim community (which makes up 5 to 10 percent of the French population). Opponents, however, protest that symbols of other faiths, such as small crosses or Jewish skull caps, are often allowed and claim that the law is anti-Muslim.

BOLIVIA
RELIGIOUS GOVERNMENT WITH RELIGIOUS LIBERTY

Bolivia is named after Simón Bolívar (1783–1830), who led the modern-day countries of Bolivia, Colombia, Ecuador, Panama, Peru, and Venezuela to independence. Originally part of Peru, Bolivia became independent in 1825. Like most of Latin America,

"The State recognizes and maintains the Roman Catholic faith, and guarantees the free exercise of all other religions."

—from the
Constitution of Bolivia

People stand in front of a church in La Paz, Bolivia, a country with a rich Roman Catholic tradition. *(Library of Congress, Prints and Photographs Division [LC-USZ62-115257])*

Church and State in Latin America, 2005

Every country in continental South America is predominantly Roman Catholic and protects religious liberty but faces controversies over separation of church and state.

☐ No official state religion

■ Roman Catholicism is the state religion

Source: CIA World Factbook 2004; U.S. Department of State, 2003, International Religious Freedom Report; Amnesty International Report 2004.

Although most South American nations have no official religion (Bolivia is one exception), the continent's religious culture is dominated by Roman Catholicism. Every single country in continental South America acknowledges a significant amount of religious liberty.

Bolivia—influenced by the Catholicism of Spanish colonizers, who, sometimes forcibly, converted local inhabitants to their religion— is largely Roman Catholic (just as the United States, influenced by British Anglicanism and other Protestant groups, remains largely Protestant). Roman Catholicism is the official religion of Bolivia, and the Bolivian government helps to financially support Roman Catholic priests.

Although Bolivia has no separation of church and state, religious freedom in Bolivia is not very different from religious freedom in the United States. Churches and religious organizations that wish to establish a formal presence in Bolivia are asked to register with the government to receive government tax and immigration benefits but are not punished for failing to register.

Bolivia's public school system includes optional Roman Catholic religious education, and students are encouraged to attend. The government is in the process of developing nonreligious ethics courses designed for students who object to, or wish to supplement, Bolivia's religious education classes.

SAUDI ARABIA
RELIGIOUS GOVERNMENT WITH RELIGIOUS REGULATION

Modern Saudi Arabia emerged as a monarchy in 1902 from the conquests of King Abdul Aziz ibn Saud (1876–1953). His son, Crown Prince Abdullah ibn Abdul Aziz al-Saud, currently leads the country.

Saudi Arabia's government operates under the conservative Wahhabi tradition of Sunni Islam, and it makes no distinction between church and state. The Saudi Arabian government pays the salaries of imams (Muslim spiritual leaders) and others who work in mosques, and regulates their behavior. The Qur'an (Koran, or Islamic holy scripture), and Sunnas (accounts of the prophet Muhammad's life), as interpreted by the Wahhabi tradition, are regarded as the national constitution. It is illegal to establish a non-Muslim house of worship, and it is not entirely clear that non-Muslim worship is legal in private homes. Although the official position of the Saudi Arabian government is that private worship is legal, non-Muslims have sometimes been arrested for private worship (though no such arrests have occurred since 2002).

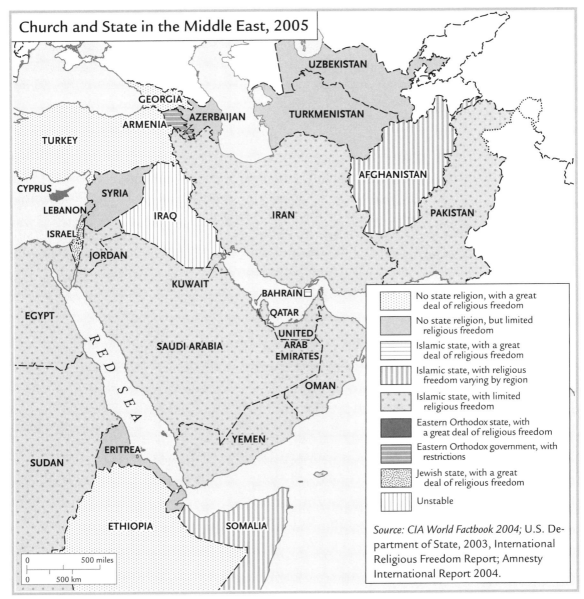

Church and State in the Middle East, 2005

UZBEKISTAN

GEORGIA

ARMENIA — AZERBAIJAN

TURKMENISTAN

TURKEY

CYPRUS

SYRIA

LEBANON

IRAQ

ISRAEL

JORDAN

AFGHANISTAN

IRAN

PAKISTAN

KUWAIT

BAHRAIN ☐

EGYPT

QATAR

UNITED ARAB EMIRATES

SAUDI ARABIA

OMAN

RED SEA

YEMEN

ERITREA

SUDAN

ETHIOPIA

SOMALIA

	No state religion, with a great deal of religious freedom
	No state religion, but limited religious freedom
	Islamic state, with a great deal of religious freedom
	Islamic state, with religious freedom varying by region
	Islamic state, with limited religious freedom
	Eastern Orthodox state, with a great deal of religious freedom
	Eastern Orthodox government, with restrictions
	Jewish state, with a great deal of religious freedom
	Unstable

Source: CIA World Factbook 2004; U.S. Department of State, 2003, International Religious Freedom Report; Amnesty International Report 2004.

0   500 miles

0   500 km

The Middle East region—consisting of North Africa, southwestern Asia, and portions of southeastern Europe—is dominated by Islam, which is endorsed by most governments in this region as an official religion. The Jewish state of Israel rests in the midst of the many Islamic nations, while several European countries bordering the Middle East are predominantly Christian. Religious liberty is not particularly common in this part of the world, though some Middle Eastern governments are becoming more tolerant. Some predominantly Islamic nations, such as Lebanon and Turkey, recognize separation of church and state.

Under Saudi Arabian law, only Muslims are considered full citizens. Saudis who convert from Islam to another faith may be found guilty of apostasy, a charge that carries the death penalty (though it is seldom enforced). Non-Muslims who are found guilty of evangelizing are subject to arrest and, if they are from outside of Saudi Arabia, deportation. Shiite Muslims, who belong to a different tradition of Islam, have also been subject to persecution.

Many Saudis disagree with the government's strict policies against Shiites and non-Muslims and have petitioned the government to change those policies. For its part, the Saudi Arabian government has indicated some interest in reform by regulating more tightly the behavior of the Commission for Promotion of Virtue and the Prevention of Vice (armed religious police that regulate public behavior to ensure it meets strict religious standards) and removing hundreds of imams from their positinos who spoke violently against non-Muslims.

The Future of Religious Freedom in America

Whatever else one can say about the state of religious freedom in America, it has changed dramatically over time. After millennia of American Indian religious traditions developing and competing with one another in ways that one can only imagine, French and Spanish explorers brought Roman Catholicism to the continent and British explorers brought Protestantism. The early colonies made no attempt to separate religion and the government. Laws were very frequently based on religious doctrines, and churches were often funded and controlled by the government. The American Revolution theoretically separated the government from religion, but even then religious freedom was not absolute and the government was allowed to endorse popular religious ideas. It was only within the past 50 years that the U.S. government was held to a standard that required it to separate from religion entirely.

There is no way of knowing for certain what tomorrow's controversies will be, but one can make an educated guess by looking at how controversies have changed or been resolved in the past. Three factors stand out.

1. **History:** The Supreme Court always bases its rulings on the law itself and on precedents, earlier cases that seem to justify its current position. While there are sometimes surprise verdicts, justices defend their rulings by citing a past history of dissenting opinions or other relevant judgments. Law is not a science that can radically change as soon as new information becomes available; it is a tradition that always relies, in some way, on the past. U.S. Supreme Court justices do not have the authority to strike

down laws just because they choose to do so; in response to a court challenge to a law, they must always justify their decision on the basis of laws (such as the Bill of Rights) or on past rulings.

2. **Politics:** Congress can pass a constitutional amendment overruling any judgment that the Supreme Court has made. The problem is that the amendment must have very strong support—it must be approved by two-thirds of both the U.S. House of Representatives and the U.S. Senate, signed by the president of the United States, and ratified (approved) by the legislatures of at least two-thirds of the states.

3. **Religious Belief:** Voters determine who is elected to public office, and the religious beliefs of voters can play a central role in determining what the government does. For this reason, a government elected by voters who identify strongly with one religion is more likely to reflect the beliefs of that religion in its laws than a government elected by voters of many different religions.

THE POLITICS OF FAITH

Over the past 30 years, the role of religion in politics has changed significantly. During the late 1960s and early 1970s, when religious leaders such as the Baptist minister Dr. Martin Luther King, Jr., and Rabbi Abraham Joshua Heschel (1907–72) actively campaigned for civil rights and against the Vietnam War, they were regarded as liberals. Other religious leaders took on a public role—such as the evangelist Billy Graham, a conservative Democrat who had campaigned for President Richard Nixon (1913–94)—but there was no united conservative movement, or Religious Right, as there is today.

The single event that probably created the Religious Right was the Supreme Court's decision in *Roe v. Wade* (1973), which legalized abortion. This created a huge schism between feminists, who tended to support legalized abortion, and religious conservatives, who fiercely opposed legalized abortion. As many Republican national politicians began to oppose legalized abortion and Democratic national politicians began to support it, some activists started to organize political movements to elect antiabortion candidates.

One of these activists was the Reverend Jerry Falwell, pastor of Thomas Road Baptist Church in Lynchburg, Virginia. Like many

"I believe that unarmed truth and unconditional love will have the final word in reality. This is why right, temporarily defeated, is stronger than evil triumphant."

—*Rev. Dr. Martin Luther King, Jr., from his 1964 Nobel Peace Prize acceptance speech*

During the early 1980s, the Moral Majority and similar religious conservative organizations encouraged millions of evangelical Christians to vote for President Ronald Reagan. *(Library of Congress, Prints and Photographs Division [LC-USZ62-101369])*

religious conservatives, Falwell adopted some views that were once considered liberal; for example, although he was a segregationist during his early life, his views changed over time, and he took a great personal risk when he began to integrate his predominantly white, socially conservative church in 1968. By the time the *Roe v. Wade* ruling came down, Falwell's church had more than 800 members and his radio show, the *Old-Time Gospel Hour,* had become extremely popular. Yet like most religious conservatives, Falwell was troubled by some liberal social issues—especially abortion. In 1979, he founded an organization called the Moral Majority in an effort to elect socially conservative candidates who would oppose abortion. He also campaigned against other causes such as gay rights, feminism, pornography, and the teaching of evolution in public schools, but abortion remained his central issue.

Political scholars believe that the Moral Majority played a significant role in electing President Ronald Reagan (1911–2004), a staunch opponent of abortion. Several million religious conservatives who

> "The idea that religion and politics don't mix was invented by the devil to keep Christians from running their own country."
>
> —*Rev. Jerry Falwell, from a 1976 sermon*

had not voted in recent elections came out to vote for Reagan in 1980 and contributed to his landslide reelection in 1984. Not all religious leaders were supportive of the Republican Party, however; many campaigned on behalf of world peace and support for the poor, and believed that Republicans were not doing as much as Democrats to support these causes.

Falwell grew disenchanted with work as a full-time political activist and retired from the Moral Majority in 1987 to focus on his ministry. At this point the organization had already begun to lose prestige, and it disbanded not long afterward in 1989. In the same year, the Reverend Pat Robertson—creator of *The 700 Club,* a conservative Christian television program—founded the Christian Coalition, a new organization that shared many goals with the Moral Majority and met with similar success. Although Democratic president Bill Clinton was elected in 1992, Republicans claimed both the U.S. House and Senate in 1994—the first time they had controlled Congress for 40 years. Part of the reason for the organization's success was the distribution of pro-Republican voter guides in churches.

The Christian Coalition has lost a great deal of influence since 1994, due in part to the government's revocation of the group's tax-exempt status in 1999 and Robertson's decision to retire from politics in 2001, but it still claims nearly 3 million members. Antiabortion activism has also declined somewhat during the late 1990s, as many political activists within the Religious Right have moved on to other issues such as gay marriage.

On the other end of the spectrum, what is sometimes called the "Religious Left" is much smaller and less influential than the Religious Right, but it still plays an important role in politics. The National Council of Churches, an organization representing 36 denominations and 140,000 churches, has regularly supported world peace and environmental causes, two issues usually associated with the Democratic Party. Also gaining influence is the Interfaith Alliance, which was founded in 1994 as a liberal alternative to the Christian Coalition. Many religious leaders—including Pope John Paul II—have also spoken against the Iraq War, which was supported by the Republican Party. Organizations affiliated with the Religious Left tend to favor a strong separation of church and state and generally emphasize humanitarian issues.

The Religious Right tends to heavily favor conservative religious values in government while defending the individual freedom of religion. Although the movement is fairly diverse, most organizations that identify with the Religious Right strongly support school prayer, private school vouchers, the teaching of creationism in public schools, government funding of religious charities, and references to God and other religious ideas in official government statements (such as the Pledge of Allegiance). The Religious Right is predominantly Christian, but its members generally affirm the importance of a broader Judeo-Christian heritage (religious ideals common to Judaism, Christianity, and Islam), such

An inscription on the Washington Memorial Arch, erected in 1892 in New York City, reads "Let us raise a standard to which the wise and honest can repair / The event is in the hand of God." Many national monuments include references to God or to other religious ideas. *(Library of Congress, Prints and Photographs Division [LC-D41-53])*

WHAT IS A RELIGION?

In May 2004, a comptroller for the state of Texas took aim at a Unitarian Universalist Church shortly after Unitarian Universalist churches in Massachusetts began performing gay marriages. The Unitarian Universalist tradition has historically centered on belief in a god or higher power but does not embrace a creed. After public outcry, the comptroller reversed her decision and restored the Unitarian Universalist church's tax-exempt status.

The comptroller was enforcing a standard that defines religion as a tradition that compels belief in "God, gods, or a higher power." Yet in addition to excluding noncreedal religions such as that of the Unitarian Universalists, this definition also excludes most forms of Buddhism, the fourth-largest religion in the United States. In order to qualify as a tax-exempt church for purposes of the Internal Revenue Service, a religious organization must meet most of the following requisites.

1. A real existence—that is, a building and status as an organization
2. A recognized creed or statement of principles and structured religious services
3. A church government
4. A code of religious rules and doctrines (In *Welsh v. United States* [1970], the Supreme Court defined a doctrine as religious if it is affirmed "with the strength of more traditional [religious] convictions.")

5. Its own history, however recent that history may be
6. Members
7. Ministers or religious leaders
8. A way of ordaining new ministers or religious leaders
9. Literature or scripture
10. Places set aside for religious services
11. A regular group of worshippers in attendance
12. Regularly held religious services
13. Classes for children
14. Seminaries to train new ministers

Obviously, many churches do not meet all of these requirements. Traditional Quakers, for example, have no ordained ministers, and many Baptist and Pentecostal churches do not require their ministers to attend seminaries. Some churches, such as those tailored to college students, do not have special classes for children. Nevertheless, this code provides general guidelines that tend to distinguish churches from other organizations for tax purposes.

Religion is notoriously difficult to define. Scholars continue to disagree regarding which traditions can and cannot be defined as religious. Perhaps the most generous definition is the one set forth by the U.S. Supreme Court in Welsh v. United States (1970): A belief is religious if it is held "with the strength of more traditional convictions."

as worship of one God and adherence to the religious laws set forth in the Ten Commandments. What politicians choose to do in the coming years will depend to a great extent not only on the power of organizations affiliated with the Religious Right but also on their constituents' priorities.

AMERICA'S CHANGING RELIGIOUS LANDSCAPE

Political scientists still tend to think of religious belief as a primarily Christian issue. The Religious Right is identified almost exclusively with conservative Christians, and the Religious Left is identified with more liberal Christians. While it is true that the United States is a predominantly Christian country, its religious identity has changed dramatically in recent years.

In 1990, the City University of New York (CUNY) conducted the National Survey of Religious Identification (NSRI), which was at the time the largest survey of religious identity in America. CUNY

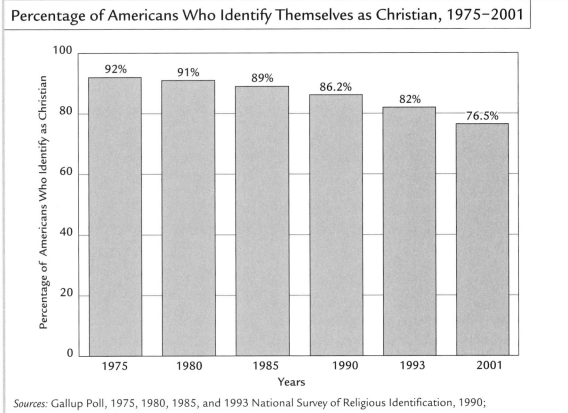

Percentage of Americans Who Identify Themselves as Christian, 1975–2001

Sources: Gallup Poll, 1975, 1980, 1985, and 1993 National Survey of Religious Identification, 1990; American Religious Identification Survey, 2001.

conducted a new survey, the American Religious Identification Survey (ARIS), in 2001 to follow up on its results. The shift in American religious identity was astonishing.

In 1990, the U.S. adult population stood at 175.4 million. Of these adults, 151.2 million—86.2 percent—identified themselves as Christian. When the survey was conducted in 2001, the U.S. adult population had increased to 208 million. The number of Christians had also increased, to 159 million, but they only made up 76.5 percent of the population. In just 11 years, the percentage of adult Christians in America had dropped by nearly 10 percent. How did this happen?

Although the overall number of adult Christians increased, the number of religious non-Christians and the number of those who do not identify with a single faith grew even more quickly. The number of nonreligious Americans increased by a huge margin and now accounts for more than 14 percent of the population, and the size of several other faiths has more than doubled. As mass media make Americans more aware of non-Christian traditions, and as immigration laws continue to bring new non-Christian immigrants into the country, the dynamics of religion will most likely continue to change. While it is impossible to say for certain how American religious identity might change in the future, Christianity's role in American religious culture does seem to be shrinking. Whether it will eventually become a minority faith—and what faith, if any, may gain prominence in its place—is impossible to say.

No religious group better embodies American religious culture's potential for change like the Roman Catholic Church. No Roman Catholic bishop was assigned to the United States until 1790, and the Catholic population in the almost exclusively Protestant United States remained tiny until the 1840s. But due to a number of factors—most notably an overall increase in immigration from predominantly Catholic European countries—the Catholic community grew exponentially. By the end of the 19th century, over a period of 50 years, the Roman Catholic Church had grown from a tiny minority faith to the largest religious denomination in the United States. It remains so to this day.

Whether American religious identity remains stable or changes drastically, it will almost certainly yield surprises. Future Americans

A photograph of St. Patrick's Cathedral in New York City. When construction began on the cathedral, in 1858, Roman Catholics were an excluded minority group. By the time this photograph was taken, in 1894, Catholicism had become the single largest religious denomination in the United States. It remains so to this day. *(Library of Congress, Prints and Photographs Division [LC-USZ62-103447])*

will most likely find themselves debating entirely new issues in religion and government—and, as history has shown, it is also likely that they will continue to argue about many of the same controversies argued about today. The 16 words that began James Madison's

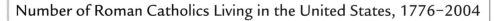

Number of Roman Catholics Living in the United States, 1776–2004

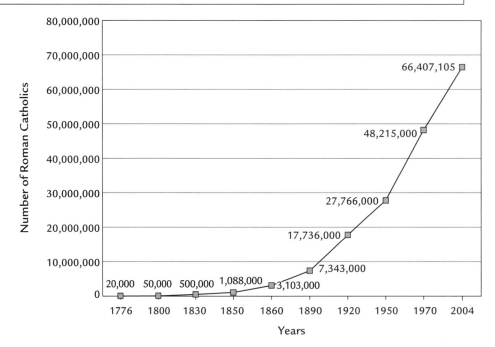

Sources: Adherents.com; H. Paul Chalfant, et al., *Religion in Contemporary Society* (3rd edition), Itasca, Ill.: Peacock, 1994; Rodney Finke and Rodney Stark, *The Churching of America 1776–1990,* New Brunswick, N.J.: Rutgers University Press, 1992; Thomas Bokenkotter, *A Concise History of the Catholic Church,* Garden City, N.Y.: Doubleday, 1977; *Historical Statistics of the United States: Colonial Times to 1970,* Washington, D.C.: U.S. Census Bureau, 1975; Eileen W. Linder (ed.), *Yearbook of American and Canadian Churches 2004,* Nashville, Tenn.: Abingdon, 2004.

proposed Bill of Rights in 1789—"Congress shall make no law respecting an establishment of religion, or prohibiting the free exercise thereof"—have been applied to countless situations that Madison himself would never have imagined. As America's religious culture changes over time, it is extremely likely that these words will one day be applied to future controversies that one also cannot imagine at present.

Glossary

accommodationism   The theory that the establishment clause of the First Amendment allows the government to support or accommodate religion provided that it does not give special status to any specific religion. Opposing views include preferentialism and separationism.

acquittal   A "not guilty" verdict.

agnostic   A person who does not firmly believe or disbelieve in God.

Anglican   A member of the Church of England (or other national churches that have affiliated with it). The Church of England began as a branch of the Roman Catholic Church but became independent in 1533. Although the Church of England is often described as Protestant, it has historically represented a middle ground between Protestantism and Roman Catholicism. After the American Revolution (1775–83), Anglicans living in the United States became known as Episcopalians.

Antinomian   A member of a group of 17th-century Christians living in Massachusetts who believed that an individual's moral conduct does not reflect his or her relationship with God and that the Bible is not as important as personal religious experience.

anti-semitism   Bigotry or discrimination directed against Jews.

Articles of Confederation   The 1781 document that created the first United States government and left nearly all power to the states. The articles would be replaced by the U.S. Constitution (1787).

Asian Exclusion League   A racist organization that attempted to discourage Asian immigration during the early 20th century.

atheist   A person who believes that there is no God.

Baptist   A member of the Baptist Church. The Baptist movement began during the early 17th century and has always granted power to local churches rather than national denominations. The most distinctive beliefs of Baptist doctrine are that baptism should be performed only on those who believe the basic doctrines of Christianity (and never on infants) and that all believers should be baptized by full immersion. In America, Baptists have historically been strong advocates for religious freedom and separation of church and state.

Bill of Rights   The first 10 amendments to the U.S. Constitution, proposed by James Madison (1751–1836) in 1789. Based on the English Bill of Rights and the Virginia Declaration of Rights, the Bill of Rights protects free speech and religious freedom (First Amendment), as well as guaranteeing protection from unwarranted searches (Fourth Amendment) and cruel and unusual punishment (Eighth Amendment). Although the Bill of Rights explicitly restricts only the federal government, it has also been applied to state law under the incorporation doctrine.

blasphemy   A statement that expresses hatred toward God or other sacred entities. Laws against blasphemy have been used to prosecute heretics and members of minority faiths.

Buddhism   A religion or way of life focusing on the teachings of Prince Siddhartha Gautama (563–483 B.C.), better known as the Buddha ("enlightened one"). According to tradition, the Buddha gave up his earthly power and riches to become a monk and solve the most fundamental riddles of life. Most Buddhists believe in reincarnation and karma (the belief that all deeds are rewarded and punished, either in this life or in future lives), but do not worship a god.

conscientious objector   A person who refuses to participate in a duty or behavior based on deeply held beliefs. The term is often used exclusively to describe pacifists who oppose war on religious grounds.

Conservative Judaism   A major branch of Judaism that originated in the United States as a middle-ground alternative to the more conservative Orthodox Judaism and the more liberal Reform Judaism. The international center of Conservative Judaism is the Jewish Theological Seminary of America in New York City.

Dutch Reformed Protestant   A member of the Dutch Reformed Church (Nederlandse Hervormde Kerk), formerly the national church of the Netherlands. The Dutch Reformed Church has historically followed the teachings of John Calvin (1509–64), whose writings also influenced the Puritans. In May 2004, the Dutch Reformed Church merged with the Dutch Lutheran Church to become the Protestant Church of the Netherlands (Protestante Kerk in Nederland).

English Bill of Rights   Written in 1689 in the wake of the Glorious Revolution, this document expanded the power of the Parliament and granted English citizens certain rights, such as the freedoms to petition the king, bear arms, and elect members of Parliament. The English Bill of Rights provided the framework for the U.S. Bill of Rights (1789).

Episcopalian   See **Anglican**.

establishment clause   The section of the First Amendment stating that "Congress shall make no law respecting the establishment of religion." Interpretations of this clause vary but can generally be grouped into three categories: accommodationism, preferentialism, and separationism.

First Amendment   The section of the Bill of Rights stating that "Congress shall make no law respecting an establishment of religion, or prohibiting the free exercise thereof; or abridging the freedom of speech, or of the press; or the right of the people peaceably to assemble, and to petition the Government for a redress of grievances." The section of the First Amendment invalidating laws "respecting an establishment of religion" is called the establishment clause, while the section invalidating laws "prohibiting the free exercise thereof" is called the free exercise clause.

Fourteenth Amendment   A constitutional amendment passed after the Civil War, in 1868, to prevent Southern states from restricting the rights of freed slaves. Stating in part that "[n]o state shall abridge the privileges or immunities of citizens of the United States; nor shall any State deprive any person of life, liberty, or property, without due process of law," the Fourteenth Amendment would eventually apply the Bill of Rights to state law under the incorporation doctrine.

free exercise clause   The section of the First Amendment stating that "Congress shall make no law . . . prohibiting the free exercise [of religion]." Interpretations of this clause vary, but the two most common are the nondiscrimination interpretation and the preferred freedoms interpretation.

Glorious Revolution   The nonviolent overthrow and exile in 1688–89 of England's king James II (1633–1701), who faced difficulty as a Roman Catholic monarch living in anti-Catholic times, then sealed his own fate by abusing his power. The Glorious Revolution led to the English Bill of Rights (1689).

Great Awakening   A radical and widespread renewal of religious interest in the American colonies, leading to greater emphasis on personal religious experience and distrust of organized religious denominations such as the Church of England. Although the movement as a whole began during the 1720s and continued until the revolutionary era, the Great Awakening was at its most acute between the years of 1739 and 1742 due to the work of revivalist preachers such as George Whitefield (1714–70) and Jonathan Edwards (1703–58).

heretic   A person who holds beliefs that are different from the established beliefs of his or her religious group.

Hinduism   The native religious tradition of India, which many scholars believe to be the oldest major religion on Earth. Most forms of Hinduism involve belief in multiple gods, reincarnation, and karma (the belief that all deeds are punished or rewarded, either in this life or in future lives).

incorporation doctrine   The Supreme Court's policy that the Bill of Rights applies to state law under the Fourteenth Amendment, which prohibits states from unduly restricting "life, liberty, or property" and promises "equal protection" in all states.

Inquisition   A court of the Roman Catholic Church, responsible for eliminating heresy. In Spain, the Inquisition was responsible for particular brutality that resulted in arrest, exile, conversion, torture, or execution of artists, intellectuals, non-Catholics, Muslims (Moors), Jews, and alleged Catholic heretics between 1478 and 1814.

Islam   A religion based on the teachings of Muhammad (570–632), whose prophecies were recorded in a scripture called the Qur'an (Koran). Muslims—those who follow the religion of Islam—generally regard Islam as a natural continuation of Judaism and Christianity and believe that all three religions center on worship of Allah (the Arabic name for God).

Jehovah's Witnesses   An evangelical Christian denomination that originated in the United States. The Jehovah's Witnesses have played a central role in the development of First Amendment law because of their willingness to oppose laws that violate their religious beliefs, such as those requiring individuals to pledge allegiance to the flag (regarded as idolatry by Witnesses) and prohibiting distribution of religious pamphlets (regarded as a necessary form of evangelism).

Judaism   The traditional religion of the Hebrews and Israel, which centers on worship of a single God. One of the oldest religions on Earth, Judaism has formed the basis of two other major faiths, Christianity and Islam. The vast majority of Jews classify themselves as Orthodox Jews, Reform Jews, Conservative Jews, or Reconstruction Jews.

Louisiana Purchase   The United States's 1803 purchase of the Louisiana Territory from France.

Louisiana Territory   During colonial times, a very large area of mostly unsettled North American territory, part of New France. It consisted of modern-day Arkansas, Iowa, Kansas, Missouri, Nebraska, Oklahoma, and South Dakota, as well as parts of modern-day Alabama, Colorado, Idaho, Illinois, Louisiana, Minnesota, Mississippi, Montana, New Mexico, North Dakota, Tennessee, Texas, and Wyoming.

magistrate   A judge.

Magna Carta   A 1215 document limiting the power of the English monarchy by granting some rights to landowners. Although it focused largely on financial issues and did not deal with religious freedom at all, it was the first true English bill of rights.

Mayflower   The ship on which 102 Pilgrims sailed from England to North America in 1620. Originally destined for Virginia, the ship was blown off course and reached land at Plymouth, Massachusetts.

Mormon   A member of the Church of Jesus Christ of Latter-day Saints. The Mormon tradition is based on the *Book of Mormon* related by Joseph Smith (1805–44), who is regarded in the Mormon tradition as a prophet of God.

Muslim   See **Islam.**

New France   The North American colonies settled by France during the 16th century.

New Spain   The American colonies in what is now the U.S. Southwest and Mexico, most of Central America, and much of the West Indies settled by Spain during the 16th century.

New World   The continents of North and South America (with surrounding islands), which were new to European explorers.

nondiscrimination interpretation   The theory that the free exercise clause of the First Amendment invalidates laws that are obviously intended to restrict religious practices but does not affect other laws that may restrict religious free exercise. This is very different from the preferred freedoms interpretation.

Orthodox Judaism   The oldest and most conservative branch of Judaism.

peyote   A hallucinogenic drug used by some Native American tribes as part of religious ceremonies.

Pilgrim   A member of a specific group of Puritans who traveled from England to North America during the 17th century. The Pilgrims founded the Colony of New Plymouth (in Massachusetts).

preferentialism   The theory that the establishment clause of the First Amendment only prevents the government from establishing a national church and does not prevent it from supporting religion or giving special status to specific religions. Opposing views include accommodationism and separationism.

preferred freedoms interpretation   The theory that the free exercise clause of the First Amendment invalidates any laws that restrict religious practices except in cases where there is a "compelling need" to do so, regardless of whether those laws were actually written to restrict religious practices. This is very different from the nondiscrimination interpretation.

Presbyterian   A member of the Presbyterian Church. This Protestant movement originated during the 16th century based on the teachings of John Calvin (1509–64). Local churches are managed by laypersons who are elected to the office of elder (presbyter).

Puritan   A member of a Protestant sect of 16th- and 17th-century English Christians who argued for stricter religious codes and simpler worship than the Church of England provided.

Quaker   A member of the Society of Friends, a Friend. Quakerism is a Christian sect, deeply committed to social justice and opposed to war and swearing oaths. It played an early and significant role in the abolition of slavery.

Reconstructionist Judaism   A major branch of Judaism that originated in the United States and is more liberal than Reform Judaism.

The international center of Reconstructionist Judaism is the Reconstructionist Rabbinical College in Wyncote, Pennsylvania.

Reform Judaism   A major Jewish tradition that originated in Germany during the early 19th century and is currently the largest branch of Judaism in the United States. Reform Judaism differs from Orthodox Judaism in that it allows greater flexibility on matters of belief and religious law, permits both men and women to serve as rabbis, and tends to more liberal on social issues.

Salem witch trials   A series of controversial trials that took place during 1692 in Puritan Massachusetts and resulted in 19 executions. The defendants were accused of practicing witchcraft.

separationism   The theory that the establishment clause of the First Amendment prevents the government from making any religious claims and from supporting religious institutions in any special way. Opposing views included accommodationism and preferentialism.

Shiite Islam   One of the two major denominations of Islam (see **Sunni Islam**). Shiite Islam does not regard certain Sunni texts as authoritative.

Sunni Islam   The largest denomination of Islam. Sunni Muslims believe not only in the authority of the Qur'an (Koran, Muslim holy book) but also in the reliability of certain texts which describe the Prophet Muhammad's life and other teaching.

syncretism   The combination of beliefs or practices from two or more religions. For example, the Native American Church includes elements of both Christianity and some Native American faith traditions.

U.S. Bill of Rights   See **Bill of Rights.**

yarmulke   A skull cap worn by many Jewish men, especially those of the Orthodox tradition.

Chronology

1649

- George Calvert, a Roman Catholic and governor of Maryland, successfully gains passage of the Religious Toleration Act in the Maryland legislature. The act protects religious freedom for all Christians within the state of Maryland.

1654

- Anti-Catholics in the Maryland legislature overthrow the Religious Toleration Act and bar all Catholics from holding public office.

1658

- The Religion Toleration Act is reinstated.

1663

- *July 15:* Charles II grants Rhode Island a new charter "to hold forth a lively experiment . . . with a full liberty in religious concernments." With this charter, Rhode Island becomes the first American colony to have no official church.

1689

- *December 16:* In England, a limited bill of rights is approved by Parliament, providing a model for the future U.S. Bill of Rights.

1775

- *April 19:* The American Revolution begins with the Battles of Lexington and Concord.

1776

- *June 12:* The Virginia Declaration of Rights is approved. One of the 16 statutes specifies that "all men are equally entitled to free exercise of religion, according to the dictates of conscience." The Virginia Declaration will influence both the Declaration of Independence and the Bill of Rights.
- *July 4:* The Declaration of Independence is approved by the Continental Congress.

1780

- *June 15:* The Commonwealth of Massachusetts approves a constitution stating in part that "no subject shall be, hurt, molested, or restrained, in his person, liberty, or estate, for worshipping God in the manner and season most agreeable to the dictates of his own conscience, or for his religious profession or sentiments, provided he doth not disturb the public peace or obstruct others in their religious worship."

1781

- *October 19:* Major fighting in the Revolutionary War ends when British general Charles Cornwallis accepts the terms of surrender at the Battle of Yorktown.

1783

- *September 3:* The Treaty of Paris is approved, marking the official end of the American Revolution and the formal recognition of the United States as an independent nation.

1787

- *July 13:* The Northwest Ordinance is passed to regulate the Northwest Territory (modern-day Illinois, Indiana, Michigan, Ohio, and Wisconsin). The ordinance includes a provision stating that "no person, demeaning himself in a peaceable and orderly manner, shall ever be molested on account of his mode of worship or religious sentiments."
- *September 17:* The U.S. Constitution is approved, despite complaints from some legislators who argue that it should contain a bill of rights. Even without it, the Constitution protects some religious liberties by forbidding mandatory religious oaths ("I do

solemnly swear . . .") and religious requirements for those seeking public office.

1789

♦ *September 25:* Future president James Madison proposes the Bill
of Rights. His original draft includes both the First Amendment
and a clause stating that "no state shall violate the equal rights
of conscience," but the latter is struck down during Senate nego-
tiations. Although the Bill of Rights is ratified, it will remain
unenforceable until the Supreme Court establishes its power to
strike down unconstitutional laws in *Marbury v. Madison* (1803).

1802

♦ *January 1:* In a letter to the Danbury Baptist Association, President Thomas Jefferson writes that the First Amendment constitutes "a wall of separation between Church and State."

1803

♦ *February 24:* In a 6-0 ruling, the U.S. Supreme Court (ruling in
Marbury v. Madison) declares the Judiciary Act of 1789 to be
unconstitutional—thereby establishing the authority of courts to
strike down federal laws that violate the U.S. Constitution.

1861–65

♦ The American Civil War is fought.

1868

♦ *June 13:* Congress passes the Fourteenth Amendment to the
Constitution, which declares unconstitutional any state laws
that "abridge the privileges or immunities of citizens of the
United States [or] deprive any person of life, liberty, or property,
without due process of law [or] deny to any person within its
jurisdiction the equal protection of the laws." Based on this
wording, the Supreme Court will later extend the protection of
the First Amendment to the states.

1879

♦ *May 5:* In *Reynolds v. United States,* the Supreme Court rules that
laws against polygamy do not violate the First Amendment's free
exercise clause.

1914–18

- World War I is fought.

1920

- In response to World War I laws banning certain forms of political speech, a group of activists forms the American Civil Liberties Union (ACLU) to challenge legislation in court thought to violate constitutional civil rights.

1925

- *July 21:* In *Tennessee v. Scopes,* a judge fines biology teacher John T. Scopes $100 for violating a state law forbidding the teaching of evolution in public schools. A year later, the case is overturned on a technicality.

1939–45

- World War II is fought.

1943

- *June 14:* In *West Virginia State Board of Education v. Barnette,* the Supreme Court rules that laws requiring public school students to salute the flag or recite the Pledge of Allegiance violate the First Amendment's free speech clause.

1947

- *February 10:* In *Everson v. Board of Education,* the Supreme Court rules that public funds cannot be used to pay for the transportation of children to private religious schools.

1959–75

- The Vietnam War is fought.

1962

- In *Engel v. Vitale,* the Supreme Court rules that public schools cannot sanction official prayers.

1968

- In *Epperson v. Arkansas,* the Supreme Court rules that laws banning the teaching of evolution constitute an endorsement of the religious doctrine of creationism and thereby violate the First Amendment's establishment clause.

1970

◆ In *Welsh v. United States,* the Supreme Court rules that deep-seated philosophical opposition to all wars is equivalent to religious pacifism and thereby qualifies draftees for conscientious objector status.

1971

◆ *June 28:* In *Lemon v. Kurtzman,* the Supreme Court rules that Rhode Island and Pennsylvania laws providing financial aid to "church-related educational institutions" violate the First Amendment's establishment clause. In doing so, the Court establishes the three-part *Lemon* Test, which it will consistently use when judging future church-state cases.

1979

◆ Television evangelist Jerry Falwell founds the Moral Majority, an organization dedicated to promoting conservative Christian values in U.S. public policy.

1980

◆ In *Stone v. Graham,* the Supreme Court rules that posting the Ten Commandments in public school classrooms is a violation of the First Amendment's establishment clause.

1983

◆ In *Marsh v. Chambers,* the Supreme Court rules that voluntary prayer ceremonies in state legislatures do not violate the First Amendment's establishment clause.

1985

◆ *June 4:* In *Wallace v. Jaffree,* the Supreme Court rules that an Alabama law encouraging teachers to lead prayer during a mandated one-minute moment of silence violates the First Amendment's establishment clause.

1988

◆ In *Employment Division v. Smith,* the Supreme Court rules that laws banning the distribution of peyote do not violate the First

Amendment's free exercise clause. This marks a shift in the Court's interpretation of the free exercise clause; instead of using the preferred freedoms interpretation, the Court will now use the nondiscrimination interpretation.

1993

♦ Congress passes the Religious Freedom Restoration Act, which demands that the Supreme Court use the preferred freedoms interpretation when judging cases that involve the First Amendment's free exercise clause.

1996

♦ *August 22:* President Bill Clinton signs the Personal Responsibility and Work Opportunity Reconciliation Act of 1996, which allows the U.S. government to provide funding to religious charities.

1997

♦ In *City of Boerne v. Flores,* the Supreme Court strikes down the Religious Freedom Restoration Act as an infringement of state law (which cannot generally be changed by the U.S. Congress alone) and the judiciary branch's power.

1998

♦ *October 27:* The International Religious Liberty Protection Act, in which the United States agrees to "diplomatic and other appropriate action with respect to any country that engages in or tolerates violations of religious freedom," is signed into law.

2001

♦ *January 29:* President George W. Bush establishes the White House Office of Faith-Based and Community Initiatives to help religious charities qualify for federal funding.

2002

♦ *June 26:* In *Elk Grove School District v. Newdow,* the Court of Appeals for the Ninth Circuit rules that the phrase *under God,* added to the Pledge of Allegiance in 1954, violates the First Amendment's establishment clause. The Supreme Court later overturns the ruling on a technicality.

◆ *June 27:* In *Zelman v. Simmons-Harris,* the Supreme Court rules that an Ohio school vouchers program does not violate the First Amendment's establishment clause.

2003

◆ *July 1:* The Court of Appeals for the Eleventh Circuit rules that the installation of a 2.5 ton granite Ten Commandments monument at Alabama's state courthouse violates the First Amendment's establishment clause. Alabama Supreme Court chief justice Roy Moore, originally responsible for having the monument installed, refuses to honor the higher court's verdict and is later removed from office.

2004

◆ *February 25:* In *Locke v. Davey,* the Supreme Court rules that a Washington law prohibiting the use of state scholarships by seminary students is not in violation of the First Amendment's free exercise clause.

Appendix

Excerpts from Documents Relating to Freedom of Religion

John Winthrop's City upon a Hill, 1630

While he was on board a ship sailing to the New World in 1630, a Puritan lawyer named John Winthrop wrote a sermon called "A Model of Christian Charity." In this sermon he presented his vision for colonial Massachusetts as a specifically and devoutly Christian colony, a vision he had the chance to implement when he became Massachusetts's first governor a year later.

Now the only way to avoid this shipwreck and provide for our posterity is to follow the Counsel of Micah, to do Justly, to love mercy, to walk humbly with our God. For this end, we must be knit together in this work as one man, we must entertain each other in brotherly Affection.

We must be willing to abridge ourselves of our superfluities for the supply of others' necessities, we must uphold a familiar Commerce together in all meekness, gentleness, patience, and liberality. We must delight in each other, make others' Conditions our own, rejoice together, mourn together, labor, and suffer together, always having before our eyes our Commission and Community in the work, our Community as members in the same body.

So shall we keep the unity of the spirit in the bond of peace, the Lord will be our God and delight to dwell among us as his own people and will command a blessing upon us in all our ways, so that we shall see much more of his wisdom, power, goodness, and truth than formerly we have been acquainted with. We shall find that the God of Israel is among us when ten of us shall be able to resist a thousand of our enemies, when he shall make us a praise and glory, that men shall say of succeeding plantations: the lord make it like that of New England. For we must Consider that we shall be as a City upon a Hill, the eyes of all people are upon us; so that if we shall deal falsely with our God in this work we have undertaken and so cause him to withdraw his present help from us, we shall be made a story and byword through the world. We shall open the mouths of enemies to speak evil of the ways of God and [all who profess God]; we shall shame the faces of many of God's worthy servants, and cause their prayers to be turned into Curses upon us till we be consumed out of the good land whither we are going. And to shut up this discourse with that exhortation of Moses, that faithful servant of the Lord in his last farewell to Israel (Deuteronomy 30): "Beloved, there is now set before us life and good, death and evil. . . ."

Source: John Winthrop, "A Modell of Christian Charity" (1630).

Notes on the State of Virginia, 1785, by Thomas Jefferson

No single figure was more important to the cause of religious liberty in America than Thomas Jefferson, who championed the idea of including some sort of religious protection in the Virginia state constitution and, later, in the U.S. Constitution. In his Book *Notes on the State of Virginia* (1785), Jefferson argued for religious liberty as a principle of good government and pressed the case that it must be secured in writing immediately, before the American people become complacent.

The error seems not sufficiently eradicated, that the operations of the mind, as well as the acts of the body, are subject to the coercion of the laws. But our rulers can have authority over such natural rights only as we have submitted to them. The rights of conscience we never submitted, we could not submit. We are answerable for them to our God.

The legitimate powers of government extend to such acts only as are injurious to others. But it does me no injury for my neighbour to say there are twenty gods, or no god. It neither picks my pocket nor breaks my leg. If it be said, his testimony in a court of justice cannot be relied on, reject it then, and be the stigma on him. Constraint may make him worse by making him a hypocrite, but it will never make him a truer man. It may fix him obstinately in his errors, but will not cure them.

Reason and free enquiry are the only effectual agents against error. Give a loose to them, they will support the true religion, by bringing every false one to their tribunal, to the test of their investigation. They are the natural enemies of error, and of error only. Had not the Roman government permitted free enquiry, Christianity could never have been introduced. Had not free enquiry been indulged, at the area of the reformation, the corruptions of Christianity could not have been purged away. If it be restrained now, the present corruptions will be protected, and new ones encouraged. . . .

Reason and experiment have been indulged, and error has fled before them. It is error alone which needs the support of government. Truth can stand by itself. Subject opinion to coercion: whom will you make your inquisitors? Fallible men; men governed by bad passions, by private as well as public reasons. And why subject it to coercion? To produce uniformity. But is uniformity of opinion desireable? No more than of face and stature. . . . Difference of opinion is advantageous in religion. The several sects perform the office of a Censor morum over each other. Is uniformity attainable? Millions of innocent men, women, and children, since the introduction of Christianity, have been burnt, tortured, fined, imprisoned; yet we have not advanced one inch towards uniformity. What has been the effect of coercion? To make one half the world fools, and the other half hypocrites. To support roguery and error all over the earth.

Let us reflect that it is inhabited by a thousand millions of people. That these profess probably a thousand different systems of religion. That ours is but one of that thousand. That if there be but one right, and ours that one, we should wish to see the 999 wandering sects gathered into the fold of truth. But against such a majority we cannot effect this by force. Reason and persuasion are the only practicable instruments. To make way for these, free enquiry must be indulged; and how can we wish others to indulge it while we refuse it ourselves. But every state, says an inquisitor, has established some religion. No two, say I, have established the same. Is this a proof of the infallibility of establishments? Our sister states of Pennsylvania and New York, however, have long subsisted without any establishment at all. The experiment was new and doubtful when they made it. It has answered beyond conception. They flourish infinitely. . . .

Let us too give this experiment fair play, and get rid, while we may, of those tyrannical laws. It is true, we are as yet secured against them by the spirit of the times. I doubt whether the people of this country would suffer an execution for heresy, or a three years imprisonment for not comprehending the mysteries of the Trinity. But is the spirit of the people an infallible, a permanent reliance? Is it government? Is this the kind of protection we receive in return for the rights we give up? Besides, the spirit of the times may alter, will alter. Our rulers will become corrupt, our people careless. . . . From the conclusion of this war we shall be going down hill. It will not then be necessary to resort every moment to the people for support. They will be forgotten, therefore, and their rights disregarded. They will forget themselves, but in the sole faculty of making money, and will never think of uniting to effect a due respect for their rights. The shackles, therefore, which shall not be knocked off at the conclusion of this war, will remain on us long, will be made heavier and heavier, till our rights shall revive or expire in a convulsion.

Source: Thomas Jefferson, *Notes on the State of Virginia* (Paris: 1785).

Virginia Statute for Religious Freedom, 1786, by Thomas Jefferson

By the time Thomas Jefferson had written *Notes from the State of Virginia* (1785), he had also drafted a Virginia statute preventing government interference in religious matters. When it came to a vote in 1786, Jefferson had other duties—he had been appointed ambassador to France, a crucial diplomatic position at the time—and advocacy for Jefferson's statute fell on his protégé James Madison. Although he faced considerable opposition, Madison successfully argued for the bill's passage. Three years later, after he had established himself as a chief architect of the U.S. Constitution, Madison would propose the Bill of Rights, including a First Amendment protecting religious liberty. Both Jefferson and Madison would later serve as presidents of the United States.

Well aware that the opinions and beliefs of men depend not on their own will, but follow involuntarily the evidence proposed to their minds; that Almighty God hath created the mind free, and manifested his supreme will that free it shall remain by making it altogether insusceptible of restraint; that all attempts to influence it by temporal punishments, or burdens, or by civil incapacitations, tend only to beget habits of hypocrisy and meanness, and are a departure from the plan of the holy author of our religion, who being lord both of body and mind, yet chose not to propagate it by coercions on either, as was in his Almighty power to do, but to extend it by its influence on reason alone. . . .

We the General Assembly of Virginia do enact that no man shall be compelled to frequent or support any religious worship, place, or ministry whatsoever, nor shall be enforced, restrained, molested, or burdened in his body or goods, nor shall otherwise suffer, on account of his religious opinions or belief; but that all men shall be free to profess, and by argument to maintain, their opinions in matters of religion, and that the same shall in no wise diminish, enlarge, or affect their civil rights.

And though we well know that this Assembly, elected to the people for the ordinary purposes of legislation only, have no power to restrain the acts of succeeding Assemblies, constituted with powers equal to our own, and that therefore to declare this act irrevocable would be of no effect in law; yet we are free to declare, and do declare, that the rights hereby asserted are of the natural rights of mankind, and that if any act shall be hereafter passed to repeal the present or to narrow its operation, such act will be an infringement of natural right.

Source: Virginia State Legislature,
Act for Establishing Religious Freedom (1786).

Letter to a Jewish Congregation from George Washington, 1790

On August 17, 1790, the warden of the Hebrew Congregation in Newport, Rhode Island, wrote a letter of welcome to President George Washington. Washington's response explicitly welcomed Jews as complete participants in American life at a time when many other nations enforced anti-semitic policies.

The reflection on the days of difficulty and danger which are past is rendered the more sweet, from a consciousness that they are succeeded by days of uncommon prosperity and security. If we have wisdom to make the best use of the advantages with which we are now favored, we cannot fail, under the just administration of a good Government, to become a great and happy people.

The Citizens of the United States of America have a right to applaud themselves for having given to mankind examples of an enlarged and liberal policy: a policy worthy of imitation. All possess alike liberty of conscience and immunities of citizenship. It is now no more that toleration is spoken of, as if it was by the indulgence of one class of people that another enjoyed the exercise of their inherent natural rights. For happily the Government of the United States, which gives to bigotry no sanction, to persecution no assistance, requires only that they who live under its protection should demean themselves as good citizens, in giving it on all occasions their effectual support. . . .

May the children of the Stock of Abraham, who dwell in this land, continue to merit and enjoy the good will of the other inhabitants; while every one shall sit in safety under his own vine and fig tree, and there shall be none to make him afraid. May the father of all mercies scatter light and not darkness in our paths, and make us all in our several vocations useful here, and in his own due time and way everlastingly happy.

Source: George Washington, Letter to the Hebrew
Congregation of Newport, Rhode Island (1790)

"The New Colossus," 1886, by Emma Lazarus

French sculptor Auguste Bartholdi, looking for inspiration for his massive sculpture *Liberty Enlightening the World,* better known as the Statue of Liberty, found it in the ancient Greek tradition of the Colossus of Rhodes. Made from bronze acquired after a military victory, this massive crowned sculpture carried a torch that symbolized both power and freedom. The American poet Emma Lazarus, a devout Jew known for her religious writings, wrote this sonnet in 1886 to honor her country's legacy as a nation of immigrants. Her sonnet, "The New Colossus," was placed on the statue's pedestal, where it remains to this day.

Not like the brazen giant of Greek fame,
With conquering limbs astride from land to land;
Here at our sea-washed, sunset gates shall stand
A mighty woman with torch, whose flame
Is the imprisoned lightning, and her name
Mother of Exiles. From her beacon-hand
Glows world-wide welcome; her mild eyes command
The air-bridged harbor that twin cities frame.
"Keep, ancient lands, your storied pomp!" cries she
With silent lips. "Give me your tired, your poor,

Your huddled masses yearning to breathe free,
The wretched refuse of your teeming shore.
Send these, the homeless, tempest-tost to me,
I lift my lamp beside the golden door!"

Source: Emma Lazarus, "The New Colossus" (1886).

United Nations Declaration on the Elimination of All Forms of Intolerance and Discrimination Based on Religion or Belief, 1981

In 1981, the United Nations passed this nonbinding declaration condemning religious intolerance and promoting international religious freedom.

Considering that one of the basic principles of the Charter of the United Nations is that of the dignity and equality inherent in all human beings, and that all Member States have pledged themselves to take joint and separate action in co-operation with the Organization to promote and encourage universal respect for and observance of human rights and fundamental freedoms for all, without distinction as to race, sex, language or religion . . .

Considering that the disregard and infringement of human rights and fundamental freedoms, in particular of the right to freedom of thought, conscience, religion or whatever belief, have brought, directly or indirectly, wars and great suffering to mankind, especially where they serve as a means of foreign interference in the internal affairs of other States and amount to kindling hatred between peoples and nations,

Considering that religion or belief, for anyone who professes either, is one of the fundamental elements in his conception of life and that freedom of religion or belief should be fully respected and guaranteed,

Considering that it is essential to promote understanding, tolerance and respect in matters relating to freedom of religion and belief and to ensure that the use of religion or belief for ends inconsistent with the Charter of the United Nations, other relevant instruments of the United Nations and the purposes and principles of the present Declaration is inadmissible,

Convinced that freedom of religion and belief should also contribute to the attainment of the goals of world peace, social justice and friendship among peoples and to the elimination of ideologies or practices of colonialism and racial discrimination . . . Concerned by manifestations of intolerance and by the existence of discrimination in matters of religion or belief still in evidence in some areas of the world,

Resolved to adopt all necessary measures for the speedy elimination of such intolerance in all its forms and manifestations and to prevent and combat discrimination on the ground of religion or belief.

Proclaims this Declaration on the Elimination of All Forms of Intolerance and of Discrimination Based on Religion or Belief:

ARTICLE 1

1. Everyone shall have the right to freedom of thought, conscience and religion. This right shall include freedom to have a religion or whatever belief of his choice, and freedom, either individually or in community with others and in public or private, to manifest his religion or belief in worship, observance, practice and teaching.

2. No one shall be subject to coercion which would impair his freedom to have a religion or belief of his choice.

3. Freedom to manifest one's religion or belief may be subject only to such limitations as are prescribed by law and are necessary to protect public safety, order, health or morals or the fundamental rights and freedoms of others.

ARTICLE 2

1. No one shall be subject to discrimination by any State, institution, group of persons, or person on the grounds or religion or other belief.

2. For the purposes of the present Declaration, the expression "intolerance and discrimination based on religion or belief" means any distinction, exclusion, restriction or preference based on religion or belief and having as its purpose or as its effect nullification or impairment of the recognition, enjoyment or exercise of human rights and fundamental freedoms on an equal basis.

ARTICLE 3

Discrimination between human beings on the grounds of religion or belief constitutes an affront to human dignity and a disavowal of the principles of the Charter of the United Nations, and shall be condemned as a violation of the human rights and fundamental freedoms proclaimed in the Universal Declaration of Human Rights and enunciated in detail in International Covenants on Human Rights, and as an obstacle to friendly and peaceful relations between nations.

ARTICLE 4

1. All States shall take effective measures to prevent and eliminate discrimination on the grounds of religion or belief in the recognition, exercise and enjoyment of human rights and fundamental freedoms in all fields of civil, economic, political, social and cultural life.

2. All States shall make all efforts to enact or rescind legislation where necessary to prohibit any such discrimination, and to take all appropriate measures to combat intolerance on the grounds of religion or other beliefs in this matter.

ARTICLE 5

1. The parents or, as the case may be, the legal guardians of the child have the right to organize the life within the family in accordance with their religion or belief and bearing in mind the moral education in which they believe the child should be brought up.

2. Every child shall enjoy the right to have access to education in the matter of religion or belief in accordance with the wishes of his parents or, as the case may be, legal guardians, and shall not be compelled to receive teaching on religion or belief against the wishes of his parents or legal guardians, the best interests of the child being the guiding principle.

3. The child shall be protected from any form of discrimination on the ground of religion or belief. He shall be brought up in a spirit of understanding, tolerance, friendship among peoples, peace and universal brotherhood, respect for freedom of religion or belief of others, and in full consciousness that his energy and talents should be devoted to the service of his fellow men.

4. In the case of a child who is not under the care either of his parents or of legal guardians, due account shall be taken of their expressed wishes or of any other proof of their wishes in the matter of religion or belief, the best interests of the child being the guiding principle.

5. Practices of a religion or belief in which a child is brought up must not be injurious to his physical or mental health or to his full development, taking into account article 1, paragraph 3, of the present Declaration.

ARTICLE 6

In accordance with article I of the present Declaration, and subject to the provisions of article 1, paragraph 3, the right to freedom of thought, conscience, religion or belief shall include, inter alia, the following freedoms:

(a) To worship or assemble in connection with a religion or belief, and to establish and maintain places for these purposes;

(b) To establish and maintain appropriate charitable or humanitarian institutions;

(c) To make, acquire and use to an adequate extent the necessary articles and materials related to the rites or customs of a religion or belief;

(d) To write, issue and disseminate relevant publications in these areas;

(e) To teach a religion or belief in places suitable for these purposes;

(f) To solicit and receive voluntary financial and other contributions from individuals and institutions;

(g) To train, appoint, elect or designate by succession appropriate leaders called for by the requirements and standards of any religion or belief;

(h) To observe days of rest and to celebrate holidays and ceremonies in accordance with the precepts of one's religion or belief;

(i) To establish and maintain communications with individuals and communities in matters of religion and belief at the national and international levels.

ARTICLE 7

The rights and freedoms set forth in the present Declaration shall be accorded in national legislation in such a manner that everyone shall be able to avail himself of such rights and freedoms in practice.

ARTICLE 8

Nothing in the present Declaration shall be construed as restricting or derogating from any right defined in the Universal Declaration of Human Rights and the International Covenants on Human Rights.

Source: United Nations, Declaration on the Elimination of All Forms of Intolerance and of Discrimination Based on Religious Belief, Geneva, Switzerland: Office of the United Nations High Commissioner for Human Rights (1981), available online, URL: http://www.unhchr.ch/html/menu3/b/d_intole.htm.

Further Reading

Dudley, William E., ed. *Religion in America (Opposing Viewpoints)*. San Diego, Calif.: Gale Group/Greenhaven Press, 2001.

Farish, Leah. Lemon v. Kurtzman: *The Religion and Public Funds Case*. Berkeley Heights, N.J.: Enslow Publications, 2000.

Head, Tom, ed. *Religion and Education*. San Diego, Calif.: Gale Group/Greenhaven Press, 2005.

Kent, Zachary. *James Madison: Creating a Nation*. Berkeley Heights, N.J.: Enslow Publications, 2004.

Leone, Bruno, ed. *Creationism vs. Evolution*. San Diego, Calif.: Gale Group/Greenhaven Press, 2001.

Mangal, Melina. *Anne Hutchinson: Religious Reformer*. Mankato, Minn.: Capstone Press, 2004.

Marzilli, Alan. *Religion in Public Schools*. Langhorne, Pa.: Chelsea House Publishers, 2004.

Melton, John Gordon, ed. *Faith in America*. 10 vols. New York: Facts On File, 2002–03.

Nardo, Don. *Thomas Jefferson*. New York: Scholastic Library Publishing/Children's Press, 2003.

Nash, Carol Rust. *The Mormon Trail and the Latter-day Saints in American History*. Berkeley Heights, N.J.: Enslow Publications, 1999.

Uschan, Michael V. *America's Founders*. San Diego, Calif.: Gale Group/Lucent Books, 1999.

Bibliography

Bureau of Democracy, Human Rights, and Labor. *The International Religious Freedom Report for 2003.* U.S. Department of State. Available online. URL: http://www.state.gov/g/drl/rls/irf/. Downloaded on April 18, 2004.

Burke, Edmund. *Reflections on the Revolution in France.* New Haven, Conn.: Yale University Press, 2003.

Carroll, Bret E. *The Routledge Historical Atlas of Religion in America.* New York: Routledge, 2000.

Djupe, Paul, and Laura Olson, eds. *Encyclopedia of American Religion and Politics.* New York: Facts On File, 2003.

Eck, Diana L. *A New Religious America: How a "Christian Country" Has Become the World's Most Religiously Diverse Nation.* San Francisco: Harper SanFrancisco, 2002.

Gaustad, Edwin S., ed. *A Documentary History of Religion in America.* 2 vols. Grand Rapids, Mich.: William B. Eerdmans Publishing, 1982.

Gaustad, Edwin S., and Leigh Schmidt. *The Religious History of America: The Heart of the American Story from Colonial Times to Today.* Rev. ed. San Francisco: Harper SanFrancisco, 2002.

Hirschfelder, Arlene, and Paulette Molin. *The Encyclopedia of Native American Religions.* Updated ed. New York: Facts On File, 1999.

Jurinski, James John. *Religion in the Schools: A Reference Handbook.* Santa Barbara, Calif.: ABC-CLIO, 1998.

Lippy, Charles H., and Peter W. Williams, eds. *Encyclopedia of the American Religious Experience: Studies of Traditions and Movements.* 3 vols. New York: Charles Scribner's Sons, 1988.

Marcus, Jacob Rader, ed. *The Jew in the American World: A Source Book.* Detroit, Mich.: Wayne State University Press, 1996.

Mead, Frank S., Samuel S. Hill, and Craig D. Atwood. *Handbook of Denominations in the United States.* 11th ed. Nashville, Tenn.: Abingdon Press, 2001.

Paine, Thomas. *The Rights of Man.* Mineola, N.Y.: Dover Publications, 1999.

Patrick, John J., and Gerald P. Long, eds. *Constitutional Debates on Freedom of Religion: A Documentary History.* Westport, Conn.: Greenwood Press, 1999.

Queen, Edward L., II, Stephen R. Prothero, and Gardiner H. Shattuck, Jr., eds. *The Encyclopedia of American Religious History.* 2 vols. New York: Facts On File, 1996.

Ruether, Rosemary Radford, and Rosemary Skinner Keller, eds. *Women and Religion in America: A Documentary History.* 2 vols. San Francisco: Harper & Row, 1982.

Tweed, Thomas A., and Stephen R. Prothero, eds. *Asian Religions in America: A Documentary History.* New York: Oxford University Press, 1999.

Witte, John, Jr., and Johan D. van der Vyver, eds. *Religious Human Rights in Global Perspective.* 2 vols. The Hague, Netherlands: Martinus Nijhoff Publishers, 1996.

Index

Page numbers in *italic* indicate photographs. Page numbers in **boldface** indicate box features and margin quotations. Page numbers followed by *m* indicate maps. Page numbers followed by *t* indicate tables or graphs. Page numbers followed by *g* indicate glossary entries. Page numbers followed by *c* indicate chronology entries.